REVELATION AND RENEWAL

Matt DeLockery

New Harbor Press

New Harbor Press
1601 Mt Rushmore Rd, Ste 3288
Rapid City, SD 57701
www.newharborpress.com

Ordering Information:
Quantity sales. Special discounts are available on quantity purchases by corporations, associations, and others. For details, contact the "Special Sales Department" at the address above.

Revelation and Renewal/Delockery—1st ed.

ISBN: 978-1-63357-243-0

First edition: 10 9 8 7 6 5 4 3 2 1

In memory of Carl Dobson,

affectionately known as "Lasagna Carl"

Contents

Preface

My parents took me to church from the time I was young. I never really thought much about it; I figured going to church was just what people did. However, when I was thirteen, something occurred to me: "If this Christianity stuff is really true, then nothing is more important." So, I started trying to figure out what Christianity was all about. (I was an odd child. Actually, I'm still pretty odd as an adult.)

I tried learning more about Christianity through my church, but by the time I was eighteen, I realized I wasn't going to find what I was looking for in church—at least not that one. So, I dropped out. I started finding some answers when I went to college at Georgia Tech. But it wasn't through school. I met a man named Carl Dobson.

Carl was in his mid-sixties and looked homeless. He never married and was a more than a little rough around the edges. He had the personality of a coach—meaning he would get on to you if he thought you were being whiny, not trying hard enough, etc. Carl would serve (Stouffer's) lasagna dinners in the freshmen dorms four nights a week to give students a break from the dining halls and to get a chance to meet them. He would put a list of hard biblical questions out on the table and tell students that anyone who could answer one of the questions would get a free supper. The students who talked with him often ended up going to one of his Bible studies. In Carl, I finally found someone who took his faith seriously and spent time truly trying to understand what the Bible actually said.

Around this time, I made some strong moves towards fundamentalism. I became a King James only guy—except I read the 1611 King James, because I didn't want all that modern liberal stuff that had made its way into later versions. I really didn't know what fundamentalism was at the time. I just knew that I finally found some people who took their faith seriously. I've never really done things halfway.

Following college, I went to seminary, because all I wanted to do was learn about God and teach people about Him. Around this time, my theological positions started to change a lot. The first big change happened when I began taking Greek (the language of the New Testament). I learned how the original documents of the New Testament (written by Paul, John, etc.) were copied and sent to other places and copied again. In modern times, we gather up all the copies we have been able to find and use them to try to figure out what was originally written—since we don't have the originals. In learning about this, I found out that the manuscripts we use for modern translations are *much* better than the ones they used for the King James. I was like, "Well, I guess I can't be King James only anymore." Learning the truth changes things.

The next major thing that happened was that I discovered apologetics. *Apologetics* is a field of Christian study that uses reason and evidence to methodically work through everything and figure out what really is true. It especially focuses on questions like "Does God exist?", "Did Jesus really rise from the dead?", and "Why is there so much evil and suffering in the world?" I told everyone who would listen, "I've been looking for something like this for ten years! Why has no one told me this existed?"

That really opened a new world for me. Up to that point, I

had pretty much just been gathering as much information about Christianity as I could find, and I went with what seemed right. That took me down some good paths (seminary), but it also took me down some bad paths (fundamentalism).

At this point, I started systematically thinking through everything I believed from top to bottom. I started all the way back at the beginning: "Is there a god?", "If there is a god, which god is he, she, it?", and "Does that god interact with us?" If there is good reason to believe something, then I'll believe it. If there is not good reason to believe something, then I'll throw it out—no matter what. I have been working on systematically thinking through everything I believe for the last thirteen years (since I discovered apologetics).

That process has led me to do three things. First, I created an apologetics ministry called *Why Should I Believe*. I lead a group on the campus of Georgia Tech (my alma mater) where students of any or no faith can ask serious questions about truth. Some of the students who come are not Christian, and yet we all have good discussions together. It's not about agreeing with each other. It's about looking for good answers together while at the same time being respectful of one another.

Second, I started a YouTube channel and podcast on apologetics and New Testament issues for those who are interested in answers to serious questions. My hope is to be able to help people who are struggling to find something like I was.

Finally, I earned a Ph.D. in New Testament from a school in the Netherlands (Radboud University Nijmegen). I wrote my dissertation on the essence of the Christian worldview from Paul's perspective. I wanted to ask: "What is Christianity at its most basic level? What is Christianity apart from any particular group's interpretation of it? What is Christianity, *really*?"

The first book I published contains the results from my doctoral research. It is the proof. This book is the explanation. In this book, I have taken Paul's thoughts on the essence of the Christian worldview and tried to show people how to apply them to their lives. With this book, I hope to be able to give you an answer to the question that I have been wrestling with for the last twenty-three years: "What is Christianity, really?"

We will begin our look at Christianity with the story of Jesus' interaction with Pontius Pilate at his trial. At first, it probably won't make a lot of sense why we're covering this, though it might be interesting to know what was going on in Pilate's mind during Jesus' trial. However, when we come back to this in the last chapter, it will make a lot more sense.

The big thing we are going to talk about in this book is the four "links" of Christianity. Christianity is like a chain—every one of its links must be strong, because if one of them breaks, the whole chain fails. We're also going to talk about how Christianity fits into the big picture—the story of God and man. And we're going to talk about how to live all this out in your daily life (if you follow Christianity, that is).

I have made this book as short as I possibly can and as simple as I possibly can. That doesn't mean it's going to be easy though. Trying to understand how all of the big pieces of the world fit together is *really* hard. But I have done my best to keep everything focused on just the most important points and explain them in a way you can understand, if you're willing to think through things a little. So, whether you're a Christian or not, I hope this book helps you in your own search for answers.

Acknowledgments

I want to thank everyone who provided critique for this book and helped make it better than it would have been otherwise. So, thank you Asa Burke, John DeLockery, Marie DeLockery, and Chinedu Ezeamuzie. I also want to thank Ben Bynum for helping me put the audio version of this book together. Finally, I want to thank everyone who has been financially supporting my ministry. This book would not have been possible without your help.

CHAPTER 1

Jesus and Pilate

Jesus just finished his trial before the High Priest and the other Jewish leaders. He had been found guilty of blasphemy—he made himself equal with God. And so, they condemned him to death.

The problem was, at that time, the Jews didn't have the authority to actually put someone to death. Rome had all the real power, and while they let the Jews govern themselves to a degree, they did not give them the power to put someone to death. Rome kept that for itself. So, in order to execute Jesus, the Jewish leaders had to get the Roman governor, Pontius Pilate, to do it. Time for a Roman trial.

In a Roman trial, there was no jury. Pilate was both judge and jury (though he may have had counselors to advise him). Similar to today, there would have been accusers who made some claim against the defendant. However, there was no defense attorney. Jesus was on his own. Pilate would have heard the accusations from the Jewish leaders, questioned Jesus, and come to a conclusion. The whole thing was done in public, but it was a pretty intimate affair. One man held Jesus' fate in his hands, and if Jesus wanted to live, he was responsible for convincing that one man why he deserved to live.

So, the Jewish leaders brought Jesus to Pilate to have him

condemned and killed. And when they did, they said that Jesus claimed to be a king. They changed the charges from blasphemy to something a Roman leader would find objectionable: claiming to be a king.

Now, there is nothing wrong with being the king of Israel in Jewish theology. Being the king of Israel was a good thing.

Romans *hated* the idea of a king. They had some kings in their early history, and things didn't go so well. So even when the Roman Republic fell (when rule by the Senate ended) and Rome became an *empire* (rule by a single man), the ruler was never called a king. He was the Emperor, or more commonly, he was called *"Princeps"*—which means "first one" or "first citizen." So, even though they really did have a king, they still avoided using the title "king" because they had such a bad history with people who had that title. So, by presenting Jesus as a self-proclaimed "king," the Jewish leaders figured they could win an emotional point with Pilate and get Jesus condemned a little more easily.

In addition to the emotional point to be won by calling Jesus a "king," there was actually a practical reason to change the charges. By telling Pilate that Jesus claimed to be a king, the Jewish leaders changed the trial from a religious matter to a political matter. If Jesus were claiming to be king, then that means he thought Caesar was *not* king. In Rome's eyes, then, he would have been considered a revolutionary. And Rome kills revolutionaries. So, the Jewish leaders presented Jesus as a revolutionary who was claiming Caesar's throne. It seemed like an easy win. What could possibly go wrong?

So, Jesus is brought to Pilate and is first charged with being the king of the Jews. Pilate then asks Jesus the obvious question, "Are you the king of the Jews?" And Jesus said, "Yes, I am." Then, the Jewish leaders started accusing him of a number of other offenses—like stirring up the people with his teaching and forbidding the people to pay taxes to Caesar. When they make those accusations, though, Jesus doesn't reply . . . he just stands there.

Jesus confesses to one of the charges and doesn't even bother to respond to the others.

Now, if you're Pilate, you've gotta be like, "Hold on a minute. Something's not right here. First of all, I'm a Roman. The Jews hate me, and I hate them, too. The feeling is mutual. So, if they really had a king, someone they thought could kick us Romans out of Israel, why would they *ever* deliver this guy to me and try to have me kill him? That doesn't make any sense."

Matthew and Mark say that Pilate perceived that it was because of jealousy that the Jewish leaders delivered up Jesus. And you might say that this was just the Gospel writers trying to make Jesus look good and make his opponents look bad. But if you think about it, jealousy really makes a lot of sense.

Jesus was a well-known religious teacher who did many things people thought were miracles, and a lot of people believed he was the Messiah. He was extremely popular and very critical of those in charge. It's not hard to see why the religious leaders didn't like him and were jealous of him. Anyone who was in power or had the ear of the people prior to Jesus would have seen their power and influence slip away over the course of Jesus' ministry. As a general rule, people who pursue power don't like to lose that power.

So, really this jealousy thing is probably not mere propaganda that the Gospel authors were using to make their side look better. It's just how humans function. If you have something that you really value, and someone takes it away from you, *you're not happy*. And when you want something someone else has or you want to be in their shoes, at least one way of describing that is jealousy. So, the charge that the Jewish leaders were jealous of Jesus is pretty reasonable.

OK, so the first thing that seems odd to Pilate makes some sense now. The reason the Jewish leaders are delivering up their king to be killed is because of jealousy. (You can see how Pilate would be working these things out in his head). But there's something else that doesn't make sense to him. There's this guy who's on trial for his life, and he's not even attempting to get out of it. He confesses to one of the crimes and doesn't even bother to respond to the others. What's up with that? Both Matthew and Mark say Pilate was amazed at this. Well, duh!

Think about it. If you were about to be crucified, don't you think you'd come up with *anything* you could to get yourself out of being literally tortured to death? And don't you think Pilate was probably used to everyone begging and pleading for mercy or arguing that they really were innocent and it was all just a big misunderstanding? That probably happened all the time. But Jesus doesn't even try to get out of it.

So, you can understand how Pilate might be confused by this whole situation and want it to just go away. He thinks Jesus is innocent anyway; he says so more than once. He doesn't want to condemn an innocent man if he doesn't have to. And he doesn't want to give the Jewish leaders what they want, because he doesn't like Jews. And frankly, Jesus kind of weirds him out. Pilate is thinking, "Probably best to just get out of this."

So, Pilate thinks of a creative way to get out of the situation. At that time, there was a custom that during the Passover feast, the person in charge would release one prisoner for the crowd. So, Pilate says, "You can either have Jesus, this guy who hasn't done anything wrong, OR, you can have Barabbas, who is a murderer." And Pilate thinks, "Alright. That should take care of that." And the crowd was like, "We want Barabbas!" And Pilate was like, "Seriously y'all?" (That's a slight paraphrase).

So, Pilate decides to *punish* Jesus and see if that will satisfy the crowd. He then has Jesus *scourged*, which is a Roman punishment where a person gets hit with a whip that has multiple ends on it with little pieces of metal and bone that tear apart the victim's flesh. This would have messed up Jesus pretty badly. Pilate was hoping this would have been enough for his accusers and the crowd.

So, Jesus gets brought back to Pilate all covered in blood and really messed up. There's probably a decent chance he'll die from his wounds. But to make it even better, Pilate discovers that when the soldiers had him, they made him a crown of thorns and put a purple robe on him—basically mocking him for his obviously fake claim to be king. In other words, they *literally* added insult to injury.

And Pilate is like, "Maybe this will be enough to satisfy the crowd." So, Pilate presents Jesus to the crowd—a Jesus who has been torn apart and then dressed up like a king. And Pilate was like, "Here you go." And the religious leaders cried out, "Crucify him!" And Pilate was like, "You crucify him. What are you talking about? This man is innocent!" And they said, "We have a law, and according to that law, he ought to die, because he has made himself the Son of God." And Pilate starts getting worried.

The thing you should know about Romans is that they were *very* superstitious. I don't say that because they believed in a lot of gods. I mean that in the sense that they believed all kinds of things caused good luck and bad luck, and you had to be super-careful about everything, or you could wind up causing yourself to have bad luck.

You know that tradition where after a couple gets married, the groom carries his bride across the threshold into their house? Well, that's a Roman tradition. It was considered bad luck if a bride tripped on her way into her house after she got married, so the groom carried her across the threshold so she couldn't possibly trip. It's kind of cute for us, but many Romans took that stuff seriously. And there was *a lot* of it.

So, you've got a superstitious Roman who was already a little on edge about this Jesus guy because he won't defend himself (which is, admittedly, weird). And now, the Jewish leaders are saying that he is making himself out to be the son of their god. If you're the kind of person who cares about your bride tripping on her way into your house and causing herself some bad luck, what do you think would happen if you crucified the son of a god?

Now, we're not talking about *the* God, mind you. Romans didn't believe in one God; they believed in a lot of gods. However, to them it was entirely in the realm of possibility for someone to be the son of a god. Remember Zeus from Greek mythology and all the children he had with mortal women? Pilate is worried Jesus could be someone like that, and the last thing he wants to do is bring divine judgment on himself. Meddling in the affairs of gods never ends well for mortals. And crucifying the son of a god is guaranteed to end badly for you.

So, you've got charges that are clearly made up, a defendant who won't defend himself when he's facing death by torture, and accusers saying the defendant is the son of a god. When you combine all these things together with a superstitious Roman who has grown up hearing about gods having children with mortals, you end up with a pretty wigged-out Pilate. Maybe he's run into one of them? And so, Pilate goes back inside with Jesus to talk with him privately and asks him, "Where are you from?" In other words, "Are you from heaven? Are you really the son of a god?"

And Jesus says . . . *nothing.* He doesn't answer. Pilate starts to become more and more unstable. He tries anything he can to get Jesus to respond—to get him to say something . . . *anything.* He says, "You will not speak to me? Do you not know that I have authority to release you and authority to crucify you?" And Jesus looks him in the eye and says, "You would have no authority over me at all unless it had been given to you from above. Therefore, He who delivered me over to you has the greater sin."

And Pilate. Freaks. Out. He is certain now that he is caught in the middle of some sort of game the gods are playing, and this *never* goes well for mortals—even in the best of circumstances. How is it going to go for him if he crucifies the son of one of the gods? So, Pilate does *everything* he can to try and get Jesus off the hook.

Pilate is now facing the crowd and trying to get them to be OK with him letting Jesus off. Certainly, he could have just let Jesus go. But this was during the Passover feast. The city has several times the number of people in it that it normally does. There are hundreds of thousands of people in the city. And Pilate only has a few hundred soldiers. His men would have been outnumbered by somewhere between 200-to-1 and 500-to-1. If a riot broke out, there was nothing he could do. He *had* to get the crowd to be OK with letting Jesus go.

Unfortunately, Mark says the religious leaders had stirred the crowd up. The crowd starts shouting, "Away with him, away with him, crucify him!"

Now, we lose something in translation here. To read it in English, it sounds just like the crowd is shouting for Pilate to crucify Jesus. And to Pilate, that would have been intimidating enough. But when you read it in Greek (the language of the New Testament), you get a whole different picture.

In Greek, "Away with him, away with him, crucify him!" reads, *"Aron, aron, staurosin auton."* There is a rhyme to it that doesn't come across in English. Here is what it looks like when you add the accents in and spell it out as it sounds: *"AH-ron, AH-ron, STAH-row-SIN aw-TON!"* You see how every other syllable is accented? If you try talking through it a few times and putting the accents in (emphasizing the capital letters), you'll notice that it also rhymes.

You see, the crowd isn't shouting. The crowd is *chanting!* They're chanting like they're at a riot.

"AH-ron, AH-ron, STAH-row-SIN aw-TON!"
"AH-ron, AH-ron, STAH-row-SIN aw-TON!"

The riot that Pilate wants to avoid is starting. The riot of people who would almost certainly come after him looks like it might happen. The people's energy is starting to rise. But Pilate knows what is at stake. The last thing he wants to do is to get on the bad side of a god. So, he keeps trying to get Jesus off the hook.

> "What has he done? He's innocent!"
> "*AH-ron, AH-ron, STAH-row-SIN aw-TON!*"
> "I have already scourged him! He's probably going to die of his wounds anyway!"
> "*AH-ron, AH-ron, STAH-row-SIN aw-TON!*"
> "He's no trouble to you! Better to take him over Barabbas—a murderer!"
> "*AH-ron, AH-ron, STAH-row-SIN aw-TON!*"

At this point, the religious leaders played their last card—and their best one. They cried out, "If you release this man, you are not Caesar's friend! Everyone who makes himself a king opposes Caesar!"

They basically told Pilate, "If you release this man, we're going to go to Caesar and tell him you let someone go who claimed that he should be king instead of Caesar." Pilate would have been killed for that. What the Jewish leaders told Pilate was, "One of you is going to die, Pilate. It's either you or Jesus. Your choice."

This hits Pilate hard, because he knows it's true. There's no way out. It's either let an innocent man suffer the consequences or suffer them yourself.

> "*AH-ron, AH-ron, STAH-row-SIN aw-TON!*"

Pilate is thinking as fast as he can. "This Jesus guy is freaking me out. Something is up with him. Who would face crucifixion and not defend himself? I mean, I know the Jewish leaders are trying to kill him because they're jealous of him. They're probably just upset because more people are following Jesus than them. But what if there is something to his claims? What if he really is sent by their god? Am I going to have a god angry at me?"

"AH-ron, AH-ron, STAH-row-SIN aw-TON!"

"What's worse: having a god possibly angry at me at some point in the future, or dying now? Either the crowd is going to riot and kill me now, or Caesar is going to execute me later. Even if I manage to escape the riot, the Jews are definitely going to Caesar. There is no way I will live if I let someone go free who calls himself a "king." How much could the wrath of a god matter if I'm going to die anyway? Besides, who knows if the gods are real anyway?

> *"AH-ron, AH-ron, STAH-row-SIN aw-TON!"*
> "Man, I'm going to get them for putting me in this situation."
> *"AH-ron, AH-ron, STAH-row-SIN aw-TON!"*
> "But what do I do about it now?"
> *"AH-ron, AH-ron, STAH-row-SIN aw-TON!"*
> "I could let an innocent man go, but then I would suffer the consequences myself. The Jews were right. It's either him or me. So, what do I do?"
> *"AH-ron, AH-ron, STAH-row-SIN aw-TON!"*

Pilate raises his hand and silences the crowd.
The chanting slowly dies down.

"Crucify him."

The crowd roars with excitement.
Pilate washes his hands as if to say to the gods, "This wasn't my idea; it was theirs."
And Jesus is led away to be crucified.

Most of us can do the right thing when it's easy. But what does it mean to do the right thing when it's hard—when it matters most? And why would we do the right thing if it costs us personally and doesn't benefit us?

This scene shows how two different people, Jesus and Pilate, answered those questions. Jesus did the right thing, and Pilate did the wrong-but-very-normal thing. But why was Jesus right and Pilate wrong? I mean, we all sort of know that's the correct answer (Jesus was right and Pilate was wrong). But *why* is that the correct answer? What did Jesus do that was so good, and what did Pilate do that was so bad? And more importantly, how do most of us end up choosing the same path Pilate chose instead of the one that Jesus chose? How can we avoid that?

In order to answer all these questions, there are a lot of things we need to talk about. The rest of the book is going to provide the foundations we need to do that.

Then, in the last chapter, we'll come back to Jesus and Pilate and talk about what the right path is and how we can follow it.

Our journey to answering these questions starts all the way back at the beginning. We have to ask the question: "Is Christianity actually true?" The answer to that question is absolutely critical to this discussion, because if Christianity is not true, then none of the rest of this makes any difference.

CHAPTER 2

The Truth of Christianity
(Link 1)

Introduction

In this chapter, we are going to talk about the first in the series of four links that make up the *Christian worldview* (Christianity's way of looking at the world). We could call these the four foundational pillars of the Christian worldview or the four key elements of the Christian worldview. However, I'm calling them *links*, because I want to communicate that like links in a chain, every one of them needs to be strong for the chain to actually do its job. If even one of them breaks, the whole chain fails.

The four links in the chain are: 1) The truth of Christianity, 2) The person and work of Christ, 3) Beliefs and actions, and 4) The Christian life. In this chapter, we are going to talk about the first link in the chain: the truth of Christianity. For many people who are Christians, this may not seem very relevant. They would say, "Why do I need to understand if it's true? I take it on faith." But ask yourself this question: "What if Christianity were false? How much value would your faith be then?"

Now, in addition to any intellectual reasons it is important for

Christianity to be true, there is a very practical reason as well. The Christian life is not easy. It is hard. It requires sacrifice. Remember, Jesus said, "If anyone would come after me, let him deny himself and take up his cross and follow me. For whoever would save his life will lose it, but whoever will lose his life for my sake will find it" (Matthew 16:24–25). [1]

The cross was a method of death by torture, and Jesus wants us to pick ours up and follow him. He wants us to lose our life for his sake. If that's the sort of life we can expect, I don't know about you, but I would want to know whether what Jesus was saying is true. I'm not just going to throw my life away for nothing. If I am going to pick up my cross, I want to know whether Jesus is legitimate. Can he really follow through on all of his promises? If I lose my life for his sake, will I really find it? Can he really give me a new life? And if I ignore him, would I really lose my life anyway? These are all really important questions, and the answers matter.

What we do in our daily lives is absolutely important, and we should not ignore it. But we cannot skip to the conclusion. Before we jump straight in to all that "picking up our cross" and "losing our life" stuff, we need to know whether it's worth it. And to do that, we need to ask: "Is Christianity actually true?"

What I'm going to do in this chapter is lay out a few arguments that suggest Christianity might actually be true. Now, by "arguments," I don't mean fights. Nobody is angry. When I say "argument," I mean an argument like a philosophical argument. I'm talking about a logical approach to a difficult question. [2]

We are going to start off by looking at two arguments for the

---

1. All translations are my own.
2. These arguments are meant to be a starting point in your search for truth. Other people discuss these better than I do, and it's very possible these will change over time. These are meant to show you how looking at whether Christianity is true (or not) is done. My explanations of these arguments are not the final word (or even the best word) on the subject. Furthermore, these arguments are not infallible. They are based on our best guess as to what God might have done in the world and what shape it might take.

existence of God. After all, if there is no God, then there is no Christianity, right? Following that, we're going to ask the question: "Is there any reason to think that Jesus actually rose from the dead? What do historians say?" Finally, we're going to ask whether it makes better sense to look at the world through Christian lenses or not.

What many people don't realize is that you do not have to accept Christianity on blind faith. Faith is good. But blind faith is bad. *Blind faith* is trusting in someone or something without having any reason to. That's dumb. On the other hand, *faith* is about trusting *if you have good reason to*. Jesus does not ask us to trust him without giving us good reasons to trust him.

At this point, some will bring up doubting Thomas and suggest that we are told to have blind faith. Here's what the Gospel of John says:

> But Thomas (also known as Didymus), one of the Twelve, was not with the disciples when Jesus came. So the other disciples said to him, "We have seen the Lord." But he said to them, "If I do not see the holes left by the nails in his hands and put my finger into them and put my hand into his side, I will not believe."
>
> A week later his disciples were in the house and Thomas was with them. Even though the doors were locked, Jesus came and stood among them and said, "Peace be with you." Then he said to Thomas, "Put your finger here and see my hands, and reach out your hand and put it into my side. Stop doubting and believe."
>
> Thomas responded and said to him, "My Lord and my God."

> Jesus said to him, "Because you have seen me
> you believe? Blessed are those who have not seen
> and yet have believed." (John 20:24–29)

When we read something like this, it certainly sounds like we're supposed to believe without seeing. So, Jesus said we're supposed to have blind faith, right? Wrong.

What we need to remember is that we're not Thomas. Thomas spent the last three years living with Jesus. If the Gospels are accurate, Thomas saw Jesus heal the sick, give sight to the blind, calm a storm simply by telling it to be calm, and even raise the dead.[3] Furthermore, the disciples performed miracles themselves (which probably means Thomas himself performed some miracles). In addition to that, Thomas had the testimony of the rest of the people he spent the last three years living with. Thomas had every reason to believe. Thomas was criticized for not believing when he should have.

The fact is that we're not being told to have blind faith. We're being told to have faith in what we have good reason to believe is true. Now, in case my explanation about Thomas didn't quite convince you that you're not supposed to have blind faith, let me show you something that should convince you. Here are the next two verses immediately after the passage about Thomas we just looked at:

> Jesus performed many other signs in the presence
> of his disciples, which are not recorded in this
> book. But these are written so that you might be-
> lieve that Jesus is the Messiah, the son of God, and

---

3. For the purpose of this point, it doesn't actually matter whether the Gospels are accurate or not. The same book that says Thomas should have had faith that Jesus rose from the dead also says that he had good reason to believe that Jesus rose from the dead. The point is that Thomas didn't believe when he had good reason to. That's what's being criticized. Jesus is NOT telling us that we should have blind faith.

that by believing you may have life in his name.
(John 20:30–31)

John says, "But these are written *so that you might believe*." The purpose behind writing about the life and ministry of Jesus is to give you good reason to believe. People are not called to have blind faith. People are called to have faith in what they have good reason to believe. And in this chapter, we are going to talk about some of those reasons. We are going to talk about *why* we should believe. In the coming chapters, we'll move on to *what* we should believe and *how* we should live as a result. But first we have to start with the most basic question, "Is Christianity true?"[4]

1. The Moral Argument

Trying to figure out whether a god exists or not would be a lot easier if we just heard a big booming voice from the sky tell everyone, "Hello, I am God." In that case, we would at least know that a god does exist, even if he, she, or it didn't have much style.

Given that that doesn't seem to happen too often, we have to find another way to figure out if a god exists. So how do we find a god? Generally, what both theists and atheists do is look in places in which we might expect a deity to be involved, and then see whether there is any evidence for such a being or not. One of those places is the world of human actions.

If a god does exist and made humans, it seems reasonable to think he, she, or it might have some opinions on how humans should live and act. So, what we need to figure out is whether it looks like a divine being cares about how we live our lives.

Typically, this is done by focusing on two questions. The first question is: "Is there anything in the world that is really right or really wrong? Or, is everything we do relative—you know, to each his own?" The second question is: "If there *are* things in this

---

4. If you would like to look into these issues further, I have a list of books on my website, mattdelockery.com, that will help you get started.

world that really are right or wrong, are they things that only a god could have made? Or, could they have come about by some other means? Could evolution, for example, have made these things right and wrong?"

Very simply, if there are things in this world that really are right or wrong, and they could have only been made that way by a god, then some sort of god must exist. If those things don't exist or they could have come about by some other means, then this argument for a god's existence fails. That doesn't necessarily mean there isn't a god. It just means that we didn't find a god using this method.

But what happens if this argument succeeds? Is Christianity true? Not necessarily. The god that this argument would point toward does not have to be the Christian God. Right now, we're just talking about a generic sort of deity who has said that certain actions are OK and certain actions are not OK. That god is consistent with the Christian God, but it's also consistent with the Muslim God as well as other religions' gods. We would have to ask further questions to narrow down which god we're talking about.

So, let's get into the argument. Is there a god? To answer that, we need to focus on our two questions. First up, question 1: "Is there anything in the world that is really right or really wrong?"

When I look at the world, it looks to me like there really are some things that are actually right and wrong. For example, it looks to me like rape is wrong. It's not just that I have bad feelings about it, or I would prefer that it didn't happen. I think that rape is actually wrong. I cannot think of a single situation in which rape would be right. It is something humans were not made to do. It goes against how the human machine is designed to function.

Please ignore the words *"made"* and *"designed"* in the last paragraph—and for the rest of this section. I'm not trying to sneak a god in the back door. I just don't know a better way to say rape is something that goes against how the human machine *should* work.

On the other side of things, I think kindness is right. Humans should be kind to one another. Even if everything went well in this world, we should treat others with courtesy, decency, and grace. But given that this world can be a pretty rough place, we have even more reason to be kind to one another. When I look at the world, it looks to me like humans were designed to be kind to one another. Kindness is something we *should* practice.

There are plenty more examples besides just these. We could say that sex trafficking is evil, and we could say love is good. You don't really hear people arguing the other way around. You don't really hear people saying sex trafficking is good and love is evil. The reason is because some things really are right, and some things really are wrong. Some things really are good, and some things really are evil.

Now, we don't always agree on what things are right and what things are wrong. Part of this is because the world is a complicated place, and the situation sometimes makes things less clear. And part of this is because all of us are a little messed up and we see the world in a slightly messed up way. It's kind of like we're looking at things in one of those fun house mirrors that's shaped oddly and makes everything look a little off.

But the point is that there are certain things (like rape) that are actually wrong, and there are certain things (like love) that are actually right. These do not change based on culture. They were not different one hundred years ago, and they will not be different one hundred years in the future. They are things that either are or are not OK for humans to do, because we only function well if we operate in certain ways and not others. Some things may be relative, but some are not.

Now, let's talk about the second half of this argument. Question 2: "Could these right and wrong things have come about by some other means?"

Evolution is the most common way people suggest we could

get right and wrong outside of a god. So, can evolution give us the foundation for calling some things right and other things wrong? Let's take a look at how evolution is said to create right and wrong.[5]

A long time ago, back when humans were much more primitive, they had to fight for their survival every day. The world was a rough place and staying alive was no simple task. It probably didn't take long for individuals to discover that if they worked together, they could survive more easily. After all, if there were a hostile predator or another human who was after you, your chances of survival would be increased if there were two or even three of you rather than just one. Life is safer in groups. Besides, when people worked together in groups, they could share resources and divide the workload.

However, with all that sharing and teamwork, it would not have taken long before people realized they needed to figure out how to actually share and work as a team. It probably didn't work very well when everyone just did whatever they wanted and looked out for themselves. There had to be some ground rules.

For example, stealing from the group is bad. Hurting other people in the group is bad. Helping other people in the group is good. The idea of which behaviors were good and which behaviors were bad started becoming important, because the group needed to get along in order to survive.

This is the basic idea behind evolution creating right and wrong. And I will go ahead and say that, yes, evolution can produce some version of right and wrong. The problem is that evolution's version of right and wrong is more limited than I think actually exists in the world.

---

5. Everything I am about to say on evolution is simply about whether it could produce a foundation for objective moral values—things that are really good or really evil. I am making no comment whatsoever about whether evolution actually happened. I am merely asking what sort of moral values an evolutionary process could produce.

The thing is: evolution has no foundation for what is right and wrong outside of what the group sees as beneficial. But what if one group didn't care whether its members hurt each other or not. Is it now OK to hurt other people? On evolution, you would have to say yes, it's OK to hurt people, because no one sees anything wrong with it. But if there is a god who says that hurting others is wrong, then you would have to say no, it's not OK to hurt people—even if everyone thinks it's OK.

We could take this a step further and ask about relationships between groups. Is there any reason that one group has to be kind to another? It would seem that there is not. After all, wouldn't one group imposing their will on another group and taking their resources be beneficial to them? Wouldn't that give the winning group an advantage? From an evolutionary perspective, I don't see how this can be criticized. However, I think there is something wrong with this; and I'll draw a modern parallel to make my point.

Is racism wrong? I think it absolutely is. However, is this not just one group competing for resources with another group? Without basing our morals on something more solid than just "what is best for the group," I don't see how racism can be condemned. And yet, I want to condemn racism, because I think it is actually wrong. But I think we need something to ground our morals beyond just what is best for the group. I think we need a god. I think we need something that can provide a foundation for things being right or wrong at all times, in all places, and regardless of what our opinions might be about them.

What I think happened is that working in groups has helped humans *discover* what things are right and wrong. But I don't think working in groups can *create* right and wrong. Some things may be flexible based on what the group wants. What time you show up to dinner varies from place to place, because customs are different. But there is no absolute standard that you *must* show up at a certain time. The point is to be polite according to whatever the local custom is (whatever is normal for that particular group).

But other things are not flexible. Rape is never OK. No one should ever do that at any time. It is not merely socially impolite. There is actually something wrong with it. Loving others is actually good. It is not merely socially polite. There is actually something good about loving others, and we should all practice it.

Here's another way to look at it. How can we say that love is good and rape is bad? We need some way to differentiate between the two. On evolution, all we have is: "Most/all members of the group don't like rape. Therefore, you shouldn't do it, because the rest of the group doesn't like it." But if there is some sort of god, it is possible to say, "The act of rape is an act against another person. It steps so far out of the bounds of acceptable human action, that it is not a mere matter of bending the rules or doing something socially taboo. It disrupts one's very humanity—both for the rapist and the victim/survivor. After all, it is not only the victim/survivor who is changed—but also the rapist. By committing this act, the rapist is actually degrading their own humanity. For all these reasons and more, rape is wrong in a real and unchanging way."

This is not something one can say if evolution is the foundation for morality. Because of how evolution bases right or wrong on what the group does or does not accept, it cannot actually say that some things really are right and some things really are wrong. But when I look at the world, I see some things that I think really are right, and I see some things that I think really are wrong. Since the only option for real right and wrong seems to be some sort of a god creating them, the existence of a god seems to be more reasonable to me. Because of that, I think that a god exists—even though we haven't yet discussed which god or gods that might be.

This is how trying to figure out whether there is a god or not works. We look in places where we think a god might have been involved and then explore around a bit. Then, we pull everything together and try to make the best sense we can of what we have found. Very simply, we're asking the questions, "How does the world look to you?" and "What do you see, and how does that help us answer the god question?" But we don't jump straight to the conclusion. The idea is to investigate the world around us in a step-by-step manner to try to come to an informed conclusion and not just give our opinion.

So, now that you have an idea of how this whole "looking for a god" thing works, let's look at one more argument for a god's existence. There are lots of these, but we're only going to look at one more. Then, we'll move on to other things that address whether Christianity is actually true or not.

2. The Kalam Cosmological Argument

The first place we looked for signs of a god's existence was the world of human actions. Another place we might look is the origin of the universe. It seems reasonable think that a god might have done some creating. So, if a god does exist, the origin of the universe seems like a good place to look for one.

The question we need to ask is, "What does the origin of the universe tell us about the god question?" Does it look like the universe has been around forever, started by itself, or something like that? Or does the universe look like it was the effect of some cause? Basically, we're asking, "Did the universe get to where it is on its own, or did it need a kick-start?"

Now, this argument can (and does) get complicated very quickly. If you're not really into science, don't worry, I'm not going to overload you (at least I'm going to try not to). I'm just going to give you the basics. Like with the last argument for a god's existence, all I'm trying to do is introduce you to the ideas. To really investigate them, you'll need to do some study on your own. This will just let you know what's out there as well as demonstrate that it is possible to methodically work through a question like, "Does God exist?"[6]

So, first things first. Did the universe begin to exist? For much of human history, a lot of people thought the universe has just always existed. But in the early twentieth century, things started to change. Einstein proposed his general theory of relativity which predicted a universe that was either expanding or collapsing rather than one that just sort of sat there. Edwin Hubble noticed that the light from distant stars was shifted toward the red end of the spectrum. This meant that the more distant a star was, the faster it was moving away from us. In other words, the universe was expanding.

All of the evidence started to point toward an expanding universe rather than one that just sat there, and the primary theory that described the expansion of the universe came to be known as the *Big Bang Theory*. There were a lot of attempts to try to avoid the beginning of the universe implied by the big bang theory, but that isn't an easy thing to do, because the evidence for it is quite strong.

What is interesting is that there are a lot of modern Christians who think the big bang is science's attempt to get rid of God from creation. But the only reason they say this is because they don't know their history. The phrase *the big bang* was actually coined by Sir Fred Hoyle (not the card guy from the phrase "according to Hoyle"—this was a different Hoyle). Hoyle liked the idea of a *static* universe, i.e., no beginning. He thought the idea of the universe having a beginning was fake science, and the only reason people liked it was because they believed in the book of Genesis. You know, "In the beginning, God created the heavens and the earth." So, he called the expanding universe idea "the big bang theory" to make fun of it.

Think about that for a moment. Some people today think the big bang theory is an argument *against* the existence of a god.

---

6. If you're interested in going deeper into this topic, you can find a few books that will help you get started on my website, mattdelockery.com.

But back when it first came out, some people disliked it because it sounded *too much* like all of that god stuff.

To me, what it sounds like is that both people back then and people now have already decided what conclusion they want. Then, after they have their conclusion, they choose which facts to accept based on whether those facts fit their conclusion. This is backwards. We need to let the facts speak for themselves and be willing to follow the evidence wherever it leads—even if it takes us somewhere we don't want to go. And I say this to everybody, not just to one group or another. We *all* need to be willing to follow the evidence wherever it leads.

In this particular case, the evidence points to the beginning of the universe. So, if the universe began to exist, the question we need to ask is: "Do things begin to exist without a cause?" In other words, "Could the universe have just started on its own, or did it need a divine push to get going?"

Truthfully, it's really hard to see how the universe could just come into being on its own. To say it just popped into existence, *uncaused* (meaning without a cause), is really to say cause and effect somehow doesn't apply in this one special case. In all other cases, if there is a cause, there will be an effect. If I'm standing on Earth, and I drop a coffee mug, it will fall to the ground as a result of gravity. The cause is me dropping the coffee mug, and the effect is it falling to the ground. We're not going to see a cause without an effect. The coffee mug will not just sit there in midair.

Now, because the relationship between cause and effect is so strong, and every time we see a cause we also see an effect, science often works the other way around. Scientists will see an effect and go looking for a cause. They see something interesting (i.e. an effect) and ask, "Hmm . . . I wonder what caused that?" They will see an effect and go looking for a cause. The question is: "Why should the universe be any different? Why would that particular effect (the universe beginning to exist) not need a cause?"

Another way to approach this whole cause and effect thing would be to ask, "What would happen if effects didn't need causes?" Well, one thing it would mean is that anything and everything could just pop into existence out of nothing, uncaused. So, imagine you're hanging out with your friend and everything is fine. Then, all of a sudden, a tiger pops into existence and eats your friend. If effects don't need causes, you might be sad at the loss of your friend, but you shouldn't be surprised that a tiger popped into existence and ate them. After all, these things just happen.

But, of course, we all know these things *don't* just happen. And if tigers can't pop into existence out of nothing without a cause, what makes universes so special? Why do they get to pop into existence out of nothing, uncaused, but nothing else can?

So, if things don't pop into existence out of nothing, uncaused, and effects have causes, that probably says something about the origin of the universe. That probably means that if the universe began to exist (effect), then something probably made it begin to exist (cause). The universe, therefore, had a cause. And that, right there, is the whole point of this argument—to show that the universe had a cause.

Now, you might say, "Hold on now. You might have shown that the universe had a cause, but you've given no evidence to say that the cause is God." And you would be right. So far, I haven't shown that a god is involved at all. I would, however, say that a god of some sort would be at least a decent candidate for the cause of the universe's existence. After all, it's not easy to create a universe. A god seems like a possible option. But perhaps something other than a god created the universe. Let's dive into that question.

Let's go back to the big bang theory and see what we can learn from that. What does the big bang tell us? Well, it tells us that all time, space, and matter were created with the big bang. Now, what makes that interesting is that if the creation of time, space, and matter began with the big bang, then they could not have existed without the big bang. Let's break this down a bit more.

If all matter began with the big bang, then that means there was no matter just sitting around ahead of time. It wasn't like there was a big pile of stuff and the big bang just exploded it outwards. No. There was no matter. There was no stuff. Matter was created with the big bang. That means that whatever caused the big bang was not made of matter. It was immaterial. It wasn't made of stuff.

The same thing applies to time and space as well. Since time and space began with the big bang, then whatever caused the big bang was not in time or space. The cause of the universe was outside of time and outside of space. So, pulling all this together, if the big bang theory is true, then the cause of the universe was timeless, spaceless, and immaterial. It was not in time, it was not in space, and it was not made of matter.

That's not the end, though. We can probably know a few more things about the cause of the universe (whatever or whoever brought the universe into being). We can probably also say that the cause of the universe was itself uncaused. That would mean that the cause of the universe is eternal—it has just been around forever. Whether it is a god or some sort of impersonal force, a cause of the universe that is uncaused would always have been there. This is what that would look like:

Uncaused Cause ⟶ Effect

The uncaused cause has always been around forever. Nothing comes before it, because it is first. It creates the effect—the universe coming into existence.

But, what if the cause of the universe was not uncaused? What if it were caused? Then, it might look like this:

Uncaused Cause ⟶ Cause ⟶ Effect

As you can see, all we have really done is back things up one step. There is still an uncaused cause, but now there is just an additional cause between it and the effect (the universe beginning to exist). But what if there were not an uncaused cause? Well, that would look like this:

... Cause$_4$ ⟶ Cause$_3$ ⟶ Cause$_2$ ⟶ Cause$_1$ ⟶ Effect

There would be a cause of the cause of the cause . . . all the way back to infinity past. There would be an infinite number of causes.

Do you see how all this works? One of two things happens. Either: 1) We hit an uncaused cause at some point, or 2) We have an infinite number of causes before the one that actually caused the universe. There is no third option.

Now, there are philosophical reasons why you can't have an infinite number of causes (option 2).[7] However, there is another big problem with this. We have no evidence whatsoever for an infinite number of causes of the universe. At this point, we're basically inventing an infinite number of things just to avoid a conclusion we don't like. Rather than invent an infinite number of things *and* run into philosophical problems as well, it seems better to think that the cause of the universe was itself uncaused (option 1).

That means whatever caused the universe to begin to exist was itself uncaused. The cause of the universe is therefore *eternal*, it never began to exist, nothing or no one brought it into being, and it has always been there. All of these things mean the same thing as *"uncaused."* Calling the cause of the universe the

---

7. In philosophy, this is known as an *infinite regress*. An infinite regress of causes is just a cause of a cause of a cause . . . going back to infinity past. Of course, while it makes sense to talk about, it doesn't make much sense to try to imagine this happening in the real world.

"uncaused cause" is simply a short and concise way of saying all of these things together.

Returning to our previous discussion, I think we can also say whatever caused the universe was "unimaginably powerful" without any real controversy. After all, anything that can create a universe is pretty powerful, and I for one have a hard time imagining what it must be like. So, I think it's reasonable to add *unimaginably powerful* to the list.

So, let's pull this all together. Based on the nature of the effect (the big bang), we have at least five things we can know about the cause of the universe. With a reasonable degree of certainty, we can say that the cause of the universe is: 1) Timeless, 2) Spaceless, 3) Immaterial, 4) Uncaused, and 5) Unimaginably Powerful. I don't know about you, but that sounds a lot like a god to me.

Now, we haven't arrived at any particular god, and this doesn't necessarily point to the Christian God.[8] What this argument does do is point toward some sort of divine creator god. That god is consistent with Christianity, but again, we haven't arrived at the Christian God yet. Even if both arguments for God's existence we have looked at are successful, what we have is a god who is the uncreated creator of the universe and who has given us instructions on how we are to live our lives.

But, while this is consistent with the Christian God, we still haven't actually made it to the God of Christianity. What we need to do now is ask the question, "Why would we think that the god we have been looking at is the Christian God? Is there any reason to think Christianity is actually true?"

In order to address that issue, we're going to ask the question, "Did Jesus really rise from the dead?" The resurrection of Jesus

---

8. Actually, the Kalam Cosmological Argument was originally created by a Muslim thinker in the eleventh century named Al-Ghazali. Obviously, he didn't use the big bang theory to show that the universe began to exist. Instead, he used philosophical evidence. However, he was responsible for the original argument and its basic structure, so this isn't a Christian argument.

is something so central to Christianity that Paul could say that if Jesus did not rise from the dead, Christianity is worthless (1 Corinthians 15:17). That means no resurrection = no Christianity. But if Jesus did rise from the dead, then at least some form of Christianity is true. So, did Jesus really rise from the dead?

3. The Resurrection of Jesus

When we first think about the idea of Jesus rising from the dead, it seems like something a person would have to take on faith (for anyone who believes it, that is). But it's actually not as hard to show that someone rose from the dead as we might think. All we really need to do is show that a person was alive, then dead, then alive again. Conceptually, it's really easy. The hard part is actually having evidence for all three of those things—and in that order. The reason it is hard to have evidence like that is because people tend not to rise from the dead.

The neat thing about Christianity is that it bases its claim to truth on a historical event. It says that Jesus of Nazareth was alive, then dead, then alive again. And a bunch of people wrote about it, so we've actually got something to investigate. That means Christianity is *testable*. That means Christianity is falsifiable. We can actually provide evidence one way or another on whether this religion is true. Cool. So, how do we do that?

Well, we could start by looking at the Gospels, since they're the most complete records of Jesus' life, death, and (supposed) resurrection. But doing that always leads to questions about whether the Gospel authors were biased, whether they made up a bunch of facts, whether stories about Jesus became exaggerated over time, and so on and so forth. What people who really dig into this question do actually avoids all of that.

The best way to answer the question, "Did Jesus really rise from the dead?" is a four step process: 1) Determine which sources contain reliable information about the events surrounding Jesus' death; 2) Figure out what facts we can know are actually true with a high degree of historical certainty (and are accepted as true by scholars of a variety of worldviews); 3) Determine what criteria are useful in evaluating any theories about how to explain these facts (such as explanatory scope and explanatory power); and 4) Evaluate competing theories to see which one explains the facts the best.

Since I am just trying to give you an idea of what's out there, I'm going to keep this short. I'm going to let you know what facts we can know with a reasonable degree of certainty and show you how we evaluate different theories about those facts. I highly encourage you to take a deeper look into the question.[9] But this overview should give you a general idea of how to go about trying to answer the question, "Did Jesus really rise from the dead?"

The facts that we can know with at least a reasonable degree of historical certainty are pretty basic, and most are not controversial. Here are some of the big ones: 1) Jesus died due to crucifixion; 2) The disciples and others believed they saw Jesus after his death (not that they *actually* saw Jesus—just that they *believed* they saw Jesus); 3) The church persecutor Paul converted; 4) James, the brother of Jesus, converted; and 5) The tomb of Jesus was found empty several days after his death.

There are more facts I could give, but these are some of the most well-founded. Of course, not all facts are equal. Jesus' death by crucifixion, the disciples' belief they saw Jesus after his death, and the conversion of Paul are accepted by just about all scholars, regardless of their worldview, because they're extremely solid.[10] The conversion of Jesus' brother, James, is strong, but there

---

9. As before, I have a few books on my website that will be helpful. Visit mattdelockery.com for the links.

10. Scholars who are Jews and atheists, for example, pretty much all agree that Jesus died on the cross. The only group of scholars that does not think Jesus died on the cross are those who are Muslim. The reason for that is because the Quran says Jesus did not die but only appeared to die (Q4:157). So, because of their worldview, they are pre-committed to the belief that Jesus did not actually die on the cross. But those who do not care one way or another (such as Jews

are not that many sources that talk about it. Everything we have points in the same direction, and it's unlikely the Gospel authors would make up a story about the brother of Jesus not believing in him, but there's not as much data as we would like. The empty tomb actually has a lot of good data, and it all points in the same direction. However, while most scholars accept it, some don't (for a variety of reasons).

So, once we get together all of the facts we can know about what happened, we try to figure out how to best explain those facts. We could try a theory like, "The disciples stole Jesus' body and then just told everyone he rose from the dead." That would explain the fact that Jesus died, and it would explain why the tomb was empty, but that's as far as it goes. It would not explain why the disciples continued to preach Christianity in the face of persecution or why many of them died for their beliefs. People don't die for something they know is false, and if they had stolen the body, they would know Christianity was false.

The disciples stealing Jesus' body also doesn't explain why Paul or James converted. Paul was still persecuting Christians after the disciples had already stolen the body. What would cause him to switch sides *and* do it years later? Also, would a stolen body really cause James to believe that his brother was God in the flesh? What would it take for you to believe your brother or sister was God in the flesh? The disciples stealing Jesus' body explains a few of the facts, but it leaves several others completely unexplained.

Some have tried to say that the disciples and others had hallucinations of Jesus, and that's why they believed he rose from the dead. That would explain Jesus' death as well as why many *individuals* believed he rose from the dead. But it would not explain anything else. To begin with, it does not explain the group appearances like the one recorded in 1 Corinthians 15:5, because

---

and atheists) almost universally agree that Jesus really did die on the cross.

group hallucinations are impossible. Hallucinations are things that occur in a person's own mind—like a dream. Dream sharing only happens in movies; it doesn't happen in real life.

Often, the reason given for *why* these hallucinations happened is that the disciples were grief-stricken over the death of their teacher and *wanted* to see Jesus risen from the dead. However, even if that made sense for the disciples, Paul didn't want to see Jesus risen from the dead. And from what we know about James in the Gospels, he didn't want to see his brother risen from the dead either. Finally, the hallucination theory does nothing to explain why the tomb of Jesus was found empty several days after his death.

Other theories are a lot like this. They explain some facts, but they leave other facts unexplained. Now, we could try to combine a few theories so that they explained all the facts together. But doing that starts sounding like we're putting theories together just to reach the conclusion we want. Remember, we have to figure out what conclusion fits the facts the best. We don't get to decide which conclusion we want and then go looking for the facts to back it up.

The theory that God raised Jesus from the dead, however, fits all of the facts. It explains why Jesus died (because he actually died), and it explains why the disciples believed he appeared to them (because he actually appeared to them). It is not hard to see why Paul or James converted, because if someone who had lived a life like Jesus died and then appeared to you afterwards, you might start to look at the world a little differently, too. Conversions would be expected. Finally, it is easy to explain why Jesus' tomb was empty—because it was. If Jesus rose bodily from the dead, then his body wouldn't be there anymore.

Again, I encourage you to look into this more deeply. I have just given you a surface-level view of the topic to show you how we can look at the question, "Did Jesus really rise from the dead?" in a factual and historical way. If Jesus really rose from the dead, then at least some form of Christianity is true. If he did not, then Christianity is false. It's really that simple.

So far, I have given you two arguments that suggest some sort of god really does exist and one argument that suggests the god that exists is the Christian God. Before we finish this chapter (we're almost done), I want to give you another way to think about whether Christianity is true; and it's a bit different.

4. Looking at the World through Christian Lenses

The last three ways we have tried to get at the question, "Is Christianity actually true?" have been very formal and rigid. In this last section, I want to try sort of backing into the question. I want to ask: "What does the world look like through Christian lenses?" If Christianity is actually true, then looking at the world through Christian lenses should bring everything into focus. If it's false, looking at it through Christian lenses should make things more blurry. So, does Christianity bring the rest of world into focus or not?

One way to ask that question is to read one of the Gospels and think through what Jesus said and did. Jesus called people to a life that is beyond what any of us live normally. At the same time though, that life sounds like the kind of life we *should* live. For example, Jesus said, "Do unto others as you would have them do unto you." How many of us really do that? It sounds like something we *should* do, but at the same time, it is more than we *actually* do.

Jesus also called people to leave everything behind, take up their cross, and follow him. He reached out to the poor, the widows, the orphans, the prostitutes, the tax collectors, the sinners, and the outcasts. He was opposed by people in power, and yet he carried on doing the right thing even though it cost him his life. That is a hard life to live, and yet, there is something about it that *feels* right. It sounds like something we should do, even if we're not quite sure we have the courage to actually do it.

That's what I mean when I say Christianity brings the world into focus. It's not about asking, "Is there a factual basis to believe that this is true?" Those sorts of questions are important, and we've spent the last three sections talking about a few of them. But right now I'm asking, "If we step into Jesus' sandals and look at the world like he did, is the picture we see more clear than our current one?"

Read through one of the Gospels (any one of them is fine), and try to get a sense of how Jesus looked at the world, who he calls us to be, and what he calls us to do. Then, compare that to how you would answer those same questions from your own worldview (or if you're already a Christian, then use a different worldview). Ask: "Who are we? Who should we be? What should we do?" Then place those two sets of answers side by side and think about which one seems to be the better or more true way of viewing the world. Which one brings the world into focus? Doing an exercise like this is one of the ways we can ask, "Does the world make better sense when looking at it through Christian lenses?"

Sometimes, you can make things fit into a theory, and everything works. But it's not very neat—it's kind of messy. To give you an example, people used to believe that the Earth was the center of the Universe, and all of the equations for the motion of the planets worked out. But some things, like the path of Mars, didn't make a lot of sense. When you look at the night sky, Mars seems to go forward, then back up, make a loop, and then start going forward again. Why? If the Earth is the center of the Universe, it doesn't make a lot of sense, even though you can make the math work. But if you put the Sun at the center of our little group of planets, everything becomes a lot neater. And we know now which one is actually correct.

So, I want to ask not simply, "Which theory makes the equations work?" I want to ask, "Which one cleans things up?" Do we have to make a whole bunch of assumptions for our theories to work out, or does everything work out pretty neatly? All things being equal, the simplest explanation tends to be correct.

I want to be clear though, this is not a trick to get you to move towards the god hypothesis. The existence of a god would certainly make things simpler. However, the existence of a god like the Christian God adds back in some other issues we have to consider as well. For example, how could a good and loving God allow the world to contain so much evil and suffering? If God cares about me, why doesn't He answer me when I pray? Aren't we going to stop needing this god hypothesis once science explains everything?

These are all really good questions. What I'm trying to get you to do is to take your current worldview (if you're not a Christian) and compare it to Christianity. Or, if you're already a Christian, I want you to take Christianity and compare it another worldview. Which one makes the best sense of the world factually and scientifically? Which one explains human nature the best? Which one makes the best sense of the world when you try it on for size? I'm not trying to get you to ask, "Which worldview do you prefer?" I want you to look at the world around you and ask, "Which way does the evidence point? Which view of the world actually looks true?"

Conclusion

We've looked at three formal arguments for the truth of Christianity and one that is much more informal. All of these arguments are really meant to get you to do one thing: Look at the world around you and think hard about what you see. Be open to whatever the truth might be—and I say that to people of every single worldview.

It is really important and really useful to have a correct view of the world. If the way we look at the world is off, things just won't work as well. A bad worldview is like looking at the world through kaleidoscope glasses. We're not going to see very well, and we're going to run into things. And no one wants to run into things. That hurts.

If we want to make our way through this life without too much pain, it's going to help if we have a clear view of what's in front of us. Now, some stuff is always going to come at us sideways and hit us in our blind spots, even if we can see clearly. But at least we can avoid the things we can see. Practically speaking, then, it makes really good sense for us to have the right worldview.

It is important to remember that Christianity claims to actually be true. It does not merely claim to be something to help us cope with this life. It does not merely claim to give us comfort about what's going to happen after we die. It does not set itself up to be a social group so we can have people to hang out with who are like us.

No. Christianity says, "Something is broken in humans that has damaged their relationship with God, with other humans, and with the world around them. This needs to be fixed so that things can start working well again." Because that's what Christianity claims, it is really important for it to be true. If a statement like that is true, then there is nothing more important in the world. If it is false, then we can safely ignore it and find something else to do with our time. That's why the issue of truth is so important. That is why it is so important to spend time thinking about the things we have talked about in this chapter. Truth matters.

So, we have now talked about the first link in the chain—the truth of Christianity. Does Christianity paint an accurate picture of the world? The next question we have to ask is: "Assuming Christianity is true, what does it say the world looks like?" In the next chapter, we're going to talk about the person and work of Christ, because (no surprise) everything in Christianity pretty much centers around Jesus. What's going to happen is that we're going to take a look at the most important parts of who Christ is and what he has done. That will give us an idea of what the world looks like from the Christian perspective. In the chapters after that, we'll move into how we are supposed to respond—how we're supposed to live.

CHAPTER 3

The Person and Work of Christ (Link 2)

Introduction

In the last chapter, we took a look at some reasons to think Christianity might actually be true. We looked at whether God actually exists, whether Jesus really did rise from the dead, and whether the world looks less blurry when we look through Christian lenses or not. However, even if Christianity is true, we're still left with another question: "What *is* Christianity?" In this chapter, we're going to answer a big part of that question.

Remember, the Christian worldview is like four links in a chain. Each one of them must be strong for the entire chain to be strong. If one of them breaks, the whole chain breaks. The first link is the truth of Christianity. The second link is the person and work of Christ; and that's the focus of this chapter.

There are seven points of theology we're going to talk about, and they're all about the person and work of Christ—who Christ is and what he has done. These are the theological foundations for the entire *Christian worldview* (the way Christianity looks at the world). These seven points are not *all* of Christian theology;

there are more than just these seven. But they are what make Christian theology unique in comparison to other worldviews.

Of course, there are other questions we need to answer like, "If Christianity is true, how should I live my life?" and "Does what we do in this life even matter anyway?" We're going to take a look at those questions and others in coming chapters, but before we can do that, we have to understand Christian theology. We have to understand how Christianity says the world works before we can understand how Christianity says we should live in it. So, let's get going.

1. Image of the Invisible God

Our first point is: Christ is the image of the invisible God. Now, right off, that sounds like some really technical theological language that isn't going to make much sense. But once we break it down, I think it will make a lot of sense. And I think it will help us understand some things most of us have never really understood very well.

At its most basic level, an *image* is a representation of someone or something else. Of course, you already know this. Think of all the images you have on your phone. Those are representations of someone or something else, right? I mean, when you take a picture of your friend, your phone doesn't actually store your friend in your phone. You haven't captured their soul, have you? Of course not. That's because an image of someone is a representation of that person. It is not the thing itself.

Obviously, in the ancient world, people didn't have phones with cameras. That's a modern thing. But ancient people did carve statues and put people's faces on coins. And some of these have survived until modern times (though the statues don't always have all of their limbs still attached). These representations ancient people made on statues or coins were called "images."

Now, just like we know that the images on our phones are only representations of our family or friends or pets, ancient people also knew that the images they made were only representations of the gods, people, and objects they were intended to represent. So, when they made an image of Zeus, they knew the image was not actually the god Zeus himself. It was just a representation of him. It was a sort of symbol of Zeus that was meant to represent him.

So, in order to communicate something about who Zeus was, people would sometimes add something to tell you a little more about him. Zeus would often be given a lightning bolt to let people know that he was the god of the sky who controlled lightning and thunder. Similarly, Poseidon would be given a *trident* (that three-pronged fish-stabbing thing that Aquaman has). This let everyone know that he was the god of the sea.

The point of all of this is that images were meant to communicate something about the gods, people, or objects they represented. And in the same way, when Christ is called the "image of the invisible God," he is being described like one of these images. So, if you want to know what the invisible God is like, you need to look at Christ. Getting to know who Christ is and what he has done will teach you something about who that invisible being you can never see (and who often feels really distant) actually is.

Of course, there is one big difference between Christ as an image and a picture on your phone as an image. The picture on your phone is just a bunch of data represented by pixels on a screen— it is a some-*thing*. Christ is actually a some-*one*. Because Christ is a some-*one*, that means as the image of the invisible God, Christ does not simply *reflect* God. Because he is a person, Christ can actually *represent* God.

You can see Jesus acting like God's representative in the Gospels. He doesn't just stand around and look holy. He does what God would do in any given situation. And what God would do is feed the hungry, give sight to the blind, raise the dead, proclaim good news to the poor, and help people become truly human. When you look at Christ and watch what he does, you get a clear picture of who God is.

Now, even though we know God by looking at Christ, it is still possible to learn some things about God apart from Christ. We certainly can know *something* about God by looking at the world around us. Assuming the arguments from the last chapter actually work, we can know things like God is a creator God who made the whole universe out of nothing (Kalam Cosmological Argument). We can know that God created humans to function in certain ways and He cares about how we act (Moral Argument). We can also know that God really does interact with humans. He has not merely created us and then left us to fend for ourselves (Resurrection Argument).

There are other arguments besides these, so we could add more things to this list. But even if we doubled or tripled the number of things we can know about God from creation, the picture is still a little fuzzy. Things like the Kalam Cosmological Argument and the Moral Argument help us draw a sort of rough sketch of God, but they don't fill in the details. They don't add color. They give us something, but they leave us with a lot of questions. And so, when Christianity says that Christ is the "image of the Invisible God," what it means is that if you look at Christ, you see the *full* picture of God.

If you want to know who God is, look at Christ. Christ is the way God has chosen to reveal Himself to humanity, and God is smart enough to know the best way to make Himself understandable to us. Instead of giving us a list of all of His attributes in super-technical theological and philosophical language, He came as a man and said, "Do you see me? This is who *I am*."

2. Uncreated Creator

The basic statement in the New Testament about Christ and creation is: "All things were created by Christ."[11] Now, let's take a minute and think through the logic of that statement. There are three different ways we could look at it.

1. <u>God created Christ first, then Christ created everything else</u>—In this case, all things would not have been created by Christ. Christ would have been created first, then he would have created everything else afterwards. So, if this were true, then Christ would have created *most* things but not *all* things. That means you cannot say: "All things were created by Christ" *and* "Christ was created by God." It's one or the other, but not both. So this doesn't work.

2. <u>Christ created everything in existence, including himself</u>—The problem with this view is that Christ would have had to create himself. Of course, to create himself, he would have had to already exist. But if he already existed, he wouldn't have needed to create himself, because he would have already existed. If this seems confusing to you, that's because it doesn't make any sense to create yourself. It is logically impossible. So, Christ could not have created everything in existence, including himself, because to do so would break logic (which tends not to break). So, this option doesn't work either. How about the last option?

3. <u>Christ created everything that began to exist</u>—This is the most straightforward way of reading the phrase "All things were created by Christ." It means that Christ created all things, but he himself is uncreated. He has always existed.

---

11. Colossians 1:16 explains this in long form.

Option 3—"Christ created everything that began to exist"—is really the only one of the three options that makes much sense for how to read the phrase, "All things were created by Christ." Christ created everything, but Christ himself was never created. He has always existed. We could, therefore, call him the "uncreated creator."[12] But what does this actually mean?

I think most people get the creator part. Christ created everything that has been created from rocks, to birds, to people, to solar systems and galaxies. Even if not everyone believes Christ is creator, the concept still makes sense to them. But the uncreated part does sound a little funny. Really, though, it's something theologians have been saying for a long time about God. God has always existed. God is eternal. He has no beginning and no end. He is the alpha and the omega.

There are many different ways we could say this, but they all mean the same thing. God did not have a beginning; He has always existed. That's what *"uncreated"* means. To say that Christ is the *uncreated creator* means that he created all things, but he did not have a beginning. He has always existed. Christ is creat-*or* rather than creat-*ion*. Christ is eternal. Even though he came to Earth as a man, he existed before that time.[13]

Now, whether Christ actually is the uncreated creator or not is another question. And whether that statement is true or not makes a difference. *Saying* Christ is the uncreated creator is a lot different than Christ *actually being* the uncreated creator. This is why it is so important to look at whether something is actually

---

12. *"Uncreated creator* is not a phrase you will find in the New Testament (NT). It is something I came up with to take what the NT teaches about Christ and package it into a short statement. There are many theological terms and phrases you will not find in the NT (such as *Trinity*). This is just like those.

13. Jesus himself claimed he existed before his earthly life in John 8:56–58. He said: "'Your father Abraham was overjoyed that he should see my day. He saw it and was glad.' Then the Jews said to him, 'You are not yet fifty years old and you have seen Abraham?' Jesus said to them, 'Truly truly I say to you, Before Abraham was I am.'"

true. That is why the Christian worldview is like four links in a chain.[14] All of them must be strong, because if one of them breaks, the whole chain fails. If what Christianity teaches isn't true, then it doesn't matter. But if it is true, then it *really* matters.

Of course, we have actually seen something like "uncreated creator" before. Take a minute and think back to the Kalam Cosmological Argument we talked about in the last chapter. We saw there was likely a cause for the universe beginning to exist, and we were able to determine some things about what that cause was like based on the effect it produced (the universe beginning to exist). One of the things we learned about the cause was that it was uncaused. The cause of the universe had no beginning; it has always existed. It was an uncaused cause.

Isn't it interesting that the New Testament teaches that the creator of all things had no beginning and has always existed? Christ is the uncreated creator. Uncaused cause from science and uncreated creator from theology. Hmm . . . .

3. Temple of God
"Temple of God" communicates two main things about Christ. He is "where man meets God," and he is "where God meets man." I know those sound the same, but they mean two very different things. It will make sense shortly.

Where Man Meets God
In the Old Testament, God was said to be present in all of creation. For example, Jeremiah 23:24 says, "'Can a man hide himself in secret places so that I cannot see him?' declares the Lord. 'Do I not fill the heavens and the earth?' declares the Lord." However,

_____

14. Remember, the four links in the chain are: 1) The Truth of Christianity, 2) The Person and Work of Christ, 3) Beliefs and Actions, and 4) The Christian Life. Right now, we are talking about the Person and Work of Christ (link 2). However, because these are links in a chain, if Christianity isn't true (link 1), then nothing about the person and work of Christ (link 2) matters.

other verses showed that God was present in the Temple in a special way. Psalm 68:16 says the Lord Himself has chosen to rule from the Temple and dwell there forever. When King Solomon dedicated the Temple (1 Kings 8), the glory of the Lord filled the Temple in the form of a cloud so much that the priests could no longer continue doing their jobs. They had to leave.

The idea behind this is that God created the whole universe, but He dwelled in the Temple in a special way. So, if you wanted to "meet" God, you went to the Temple. The Temple is where heaven and earth connected. It is where God's space and humanity's space came together—like two roads that meet at an intersection. God operates in a different world than we humans do. So, if you wanted to "meet" God, you needed to go where God's world met our world. And that place was the Temple.

Now, meeting God at the Temple was not a simple process. It wasn't just like going over to your friend's house, knocking on the door, and going in. In order to even be able to enter God's space, the Temple, you had to make the appropriate sacrifice. Humans are sinful; God is holy. Without a sacrifice, humans cannot come near to God. Even the way the Temple is set up communicates this. Everything outside the Temple is just the regular, sinful, unholy world. But as you move further and further into the Temple, the spaces get progressively more holy, until you get to the *Holy of Holies*—where God's presence dwelled. This is where God's space met man's space.

Now, where this language about the Temple gets interesting is that the New Testament speaks of Christ like the Old Testament spoke of the Temple. "Because in him [Christ] all the fullness of deity dwells bodily" (Colossians 2:9). God dwells *in* Christ. God is still present in the whole world, but He dwells in Christ in a special way. So, instead of continuing to dwell in a building, God has chosen to dwell in a person, Christ. That means that if you want to "meet" God, you need to "meet" Him in Christ.

Now, nothing has changed since the Old Testament—sinful

humans cannot simply approach a holy God. A sacrifice still has to be made. In the New Testament, though, that sacrifice is Christ himself. His sacrifice allows humans to approach God, but it does something the Old Testament sacrifices could not do. Christ's sacrifice actually fixes what is wrong with sinful humans and begins to renew us into the beautiful and holy creations we were meant to be. The next few chapters will explain what that means.

For now, just remember that like the Temple, Christ is the place where man goes to meet God. And because of Christ's sacrifice, sinful man is actually able to approach the holy God.

Where God Meets Man

Now, not only is Christ the place where man meets God; he is also the place where God meets man. Calling Christ the "Temple of God" is one of the starting points for a big part of Christian theology: Christ's relationship to God. Theologians speak of the *Trinity* (one divine nature having three persons: Father, Son, and Holy Spirit) and the *Incarnation* (both the divine nature and a human nature joining in a single, human person). The language used to explain how this works gets technical really quickly. Don't worry, though, we're not going there. Instead, we're going to start a little further back—with some pictures.

You see, there are two basic ways Christians talk about complex theological topics. There is the Hebrew way, and there is the Greek way. The Hebrew way is more picture-based. The Old Testament might describe God as a rock or a consuming fire. Of course, everybody knew that God wasn't *really* a rock and wasn't *really* fire. These are just ways of describing God using word pictures. If someone tells you God is a rock, you get the basic idea. God is strong. God can be relied upon.

The other way Christians describe complex theological topics is the Greek way. Instead of using pictures, the language is much more philosophical. So, rather than calling God a rock, the Christian might say something like, "God has the ability to be causally active at any point in the spatiotemporal universe, and there are no powers (personal or impersonal) who can resist His causal actions. God will act in such a way as to bring about the ends He desires—especially for those whom He describes as His people." Nice and simple, right?

The thing is, both the pictorial and philosophical ways of describing God and His actions get at the same reality, even though they do it in very different ways. The pictorial (Hebrew) way is much easier for people to grasp than the philosophical (Greek) way. And it's easy to see why people talked about God in word pictures before they talked about Him in philosophical language. It's not just because word pictures are easier but because the philosophical language seeks to answer questions about the pictorial language. Now, let's go back to the Temple of God and talk about how all of this works out.

What we see in the description of Christ as the Temple of God is language about the Incarnation. God dwells in a human, Christ, just like He dwelled in the Temple. This is where thought about the Incarnation originated. All of the complicated philosophical language that came later explains how this actually works. It is meant to answer questions like: "How can a person be both divine and human at the same time?", "Is that even possible?", and "Aren't you just one or the other?"

The New Testament tells us that God dwells in Christ in the same way He dwelled in the Temple. This is describing how God and man meet—how the divine and the human come together in one person. Later philosophical language explains how this works, but the point of both is the same: Christ is where God and man meet.

Bonus Theology—The Trinity
This section on the Trinity isn't actually related to the Temple of God, but now that we've talked about the difference between pictorial and philosophical language, I can point out something

we passed over. You can actually see the beginnings of Christian thought on the Trinity by combining the last two sections: "Image of the Invisible God" and "Uncreated Creator."

The phrase *"uncreated creator"* points towards Christ's divinity (the fact that he is God). After all, who else but a divine being would be uncreated (exist from eternity past)? If you're a personal being who has existed from eternity past, then you're a god. The word *"god"* is simply the word humans use to describe that kind of being.

And yet, even though Christ is the uncreated creator, he is not the same as the invisible God (*God the Father* in Christian theology). If he were, there would be no reason to call him the *image* of the invisible God. He would just be called God. Full stop.

Remember, an image is a reflection or representation of someone or something else. The images on your phone are representations of people and places in real life. They aren't actually those people or places. When you look at yourself in a mirror, you're looking at a reflection of yourself. It isn't actually yourself you see, it is a reflection of you. Someone standing nearby might be able to see both you and your reflection (depending on the angle of the mirror). One is you, and one is your reflection. They are not the same thing.

So, when Christ is called the "image of the invisible God," he is being called the "reflection" or "representation" of God. That shows he is distinct from God; he is not exactly the same as God.

Now, when you put these two points side by side, you have the beginnings of the Trinity. Christ is both God (*uncreated creator*) and distinct from God, because he reflects God (*image of the invisible God*).[15] This is a very clear and simple way of explaining

---

15. Technically, since we're only talking about two persons, what we really have here is *binitarian* thought ("bi" for two) instead of *trinitarian* thought ("tri" for three). To make it trinitarian thought, we would need to add in the Holy Spirit. Now, the Holy Spirit is not being excluded; He just isn't being discussed here. So, this is binitarian thought that leads to and is consistent with trinitarian

what the Trinity is all about. Christ is both God and distinct from God.

Just like with the pictorial description of Christ as the Temple of God, the theology started very simply. Then, people started to ask questions like: "If Christ is distinct from God, isn't he just an additional god? Are we saying we believe in multiple gods, now? But if Christ is not an additional god, how is he not just the same as God? How is he actually distinct?" The philosophical language of "persons" and "natures" was invented later to help answer these sorts of questions. Getting into that is a much larger topic. But what I wanted you to see is that the basics of the Trinity were present right from the beginning—Christ is both God and distinct from God.

4. Firstborn from the Dead

Saying that Christ is the *firstborn from the dead* means simply that he was the first person to rise from the dead. But he would not be the last.

Prior to Jesus' resurrection, there were other people who *temporarily* rose from the dead because someone like Elijah (1 Kings 17) or Jesus himself (John 11) performed a miracle. However, all of these people would die again later. The widow's son raised by Elijah was not hanging around in Jesus' day, and neither the widow's son nor Lazarus (the man Jesus raised) are around today. They were *temporarily* raised from the dead, but they would die again later. Jesus was different. He was the first person to pass through death and come out the other side.

Christianity teaches that Christ is the firstborn from the dead. One of the reasons this matters is because it fixes a problem we discussed in the last section, "The Temple of God." Sinful man cannot just approach a holy God. There must be a sacrifice. However, the sacrifices in the Old Testament worked for a

---

thought.

limited time only. They allowed humans to approach God for a little while, but they had to make those sacrifices every time they went to the Temple. That's because those sacrifices didn't actually fix what is wrong with humans. Christ's sacrifice does.

So, what is wrong with humans, and what does Christ's resurrection do to fix it? In the next few sections, we're going to answer that question. But before we can do that, we need to talk about a topic that seems unrelated at first but is actually inseparable from Christ's resurrection. We need to talk about hope.

When Christianity talks about "hope," it does not mean what the rest of the world means. The rest of the world thinks of *hope* as a "feeling of hopefulness" or "wishful thinking about what the future might bring." This is *not* what Christianity means by hope.

Christian hope is not an abstract thing; it is a concrete thing. When New Testament authors like Paul talk about hope, what they mean is that because of what Christ has done, the future is now different. In other words, the way things actually *will be* has changed. It is not merely that we wish for them to change or that we long for them to change. They have *already* changed.

Because Christ actually died and rose from dead, a new and better future is waiting for us, and that future is certain. And because that future is certain, it is possible to have a different outlook on what's happening right now. It is possible for us to legitimately feel better about the present, because the future is different. It's not just wishful thinking.

Understanding "hope" will help make sense of many other things in Christian theology. Christianity teaches that Christians *have* died and risen with Christ, i.e., it's already happened. On the surface, this makes no sense, because you don't see many stories on the news about someone becoming a Christian, dying, and then coming back to life a little while later. The reason you don't hear things like that is because Christians have not literally died and risen with Christ—at least not yet.

Christians dying and rising with Christ is tied up with the

hope we just talked about. It is about a new future reality. Because of what Christ has done, the future is now different than it was before. Christ died, rose from the dead, and promised to take those of us who follow him with him. One day, after we physically die, we will be resurrected/raised to new life with Christ. Christian hope is about our new future reality: resurrection with Christ. Now, pay attention to this next point, because it will explain quite a bit about Christian theology and the mindset of Christians.

Because Christians know for certain that something in the future is going to happen, we speak of it in the past tense. Because we know we will one day die and rise with Christ, we talk about dying and rising with Christ *like it has already happened.* When God says something will take place in the future, we can absolutely count on it taking place. He is both capable of making that thing happen, and He is not going to go back on His word. God does not lie. Because of that, it is normal in Christian theology to speak of the future in the past tense *if* it is based on something God has promised to do.

Christ is the firstborn from the dead. He actually died, and he actually rose from the dead. The reason he did this was so he could take other people with him. Like everybody else, those who follow Christ will die one day. Unlike everybody else, those who follow Christ will be resurrected to new life. This resurrection to new life is what Christianity means by *"hope."* Our future resurrection is certain, and that is our "hope." The entire rest of this book is essentially an extended discussion of what Christ's resurrection means for humanity.

5. Beginner of a New Humanity

A little while back, someone said something to me that describes humans better than anything I've ever heard before. He said, "Everyone is beautiful, and everyone is broken." I think that's really it. The problem is we tend to focus too much on one or the other. If we only focus on "everyone is beautiful," then we miss the fact that we're all just a little messed up. After all, nobody's perfect. And it does us no good to pretend we are perfect and ignore our problems, because problems only get worse over time if we don't deal with them.

On the other hand, if we only focus on "everyone is broken," we will see God as harsh and judgmental and ready to squash anybody who doesn't measure up. That's not God. After all, Christ died on a cross (which was literal death by torture) *for us*. He knew we were broken ahead of time. That's why he died. And yet, he was still willing to sacrifice himself to help us. That is the opposite of squashing anyone who doesn't measure up. And since Christ is the image of the invisible God, that means we can know what God is like by looking at Christ. So, if Christ isn't harsh and judgmental, then God isn't harsh and judgmental.

Everybody is beautiful *and* everybody is broken. We are all *both* of those things. The reason why Christ's resurrection matters to us is that it fixes our broken parts and makes our beautiful parts shine even more brightly. We were made in God's image. Just like Christ is the image of the invisible God, we were also made in God's image (though with more limitations than Christ). We, too, were meant to reflect the divine.

Here's the problem: I don't know about you, but when I look in the mirror, I don't see a lot of divinity. When I think about how I live my life, there are some parts that I think look pretty good, but then there are other parts that look pretty awful. And I think anyone who is honest with themselves will be in a similar position. Some parts of us are beautiful, but there are also some parts we would rather people just not know about—because they're straight up ugly. Renewing us into the image of God is about fixing what is broken in us and making the beautiful parts shine even more brightly.

Another way of saying we are being renewed into the image of God is to say we are being remade into people who are truly human. We were made in God's image. We were made to reflect God. That's what it means to be human. But if we have to be *renewed* into God's image, then that means we are not in His image right now—at least not fully. We only *somewhat* reflect God. That's why we're both beautiful *and* broken instead of just beautiful or just broken.

However, if we were made to reflect God, then we are never more truly human than when we are living in a manner that reflects Him. So, when the New Testament says we are being renewed into God's image, what that means at its most basic level is that we are being renewed into true humans.

At present, we are all less than fully human. Now, we're still humans; we're not merely animals. However, because we still fall short of God's image, we still fall short of true humanity. What Christ has done is to begin to renew those humans who follow him into God's image. But since humanity was always intended to be in God's image, Christ is actually renewing us into true humanity. We are never more human than when we live and act in a manner that reflects God.

Let's put this together with some of what we talked about in the last few sections. With his resurrection, Christ passed through death and into new life. For those of us who follow Christ, not only does that mean we can approach a holy God, it also means we will be renewed into God's image. We will one day reflect God just like Christ reflects God (albeit in a more limited way). Remember how you can know what God is like by looking at Christ? Well, one day people will be able to know what God is like by looking at us. This is what it means to be truly human, and this is where we're headed.

We're not there yet though. Becoming renewed in the image of God is a process that begins in this life and is completed with the next life. We will one day be fully renewed. All our broken parts will be fixed, and all our beautiful parts will be polished to a bright shine. For now though, we are still in the process of being renewed.

6. Head of the Body, the Church

At this point, a couple themes we have talked about come together. First, if a *person* is an image of someone, it means something more than if an *object* is an image of someone. Second, those of us who follow Christ are being remade in God's image. Those may seem like separate ideas on the surface, but they're really not. Let's go over some of this image stuff again, because once we do, I think you'll see how these two ideas connect.

An object as an image can communicate information about someone. It can tell you what the person looks like—such as with an image of Caesar on a coin. Or, it can communicate something about the personality or character of someone—like how Zeus' lightning bolt communicates that he is the god of the sky who controls lightning and thunder. Objects as images can communicate information about someone, but that's really where it stops.

However, a person as an image can do a lot more than an object can, because a person is alive. Christ as the image of the invisible God lets us know what God is like in a dynamic way, because we can see him in real life situations. He's not a painting that communicates something about God but otherwise just sits there. No, he's an actual person. And because Christ is an actual person who was involved in real-life situations, he can actually act on God's behalf. In other words, Christ doesn't just reflect God, he *represents* God. Not only can we know something about God by watching Christ, God can interact with us through His representative, Christ.

Take a look at some of the things Jesus did in the Gospels. Jesus acted on God's behalf when a paralyzed man was brought to him and he forgave that man's sins. Jesus acted on God's behalf when he sent his disciples out as fishers of men to gather together those who would respond to God's call. And Jesus acted on God's behalf when he proclaimed judgment on Israel. Jesus healed, gathered, and judged people as if he were acting on God's behalf—which he was. Jesus is the image of the invisible God. And because he is a person, Jesus represents the one he reflects.

Now, here is where all of this gets really interesting. Humans were also made in the image of God. We were created to act on God's behalf. We were created to act in the world as He would act. Just like Christ acted on God's behalf, we are supposed to act on God's behalf (again, on a more limited scale than Christ).

This is the idea behind calling Christ the "head of the body, the Church." Christ is the head, and the Church is the body. The head provides the direction, and the body performs the actions. In other words, Christians are the hands and feet of Christ in the world. We are to act as he would act.

However, before we jump right in to doing things in the world around us with God's authority, we need to take a *big* pause. We should remember what we talked about in the last section: Everyone is beautiful, *and* everyone is broken. The second part of that statement should slow us down a little. Given that we are all broken, we should hesitate before thinking everything we do is pure gold—because it's not. A little humility would be good at this point. (Actually, a lot of humility would be good at this point).

We were created to represent God, but that doesn't mean we're actually good at it. That's why we have to be *renewed* into the image of God. We only partially reflect Him right now. Some of the things we do look like God, and some of them don't. To actually represent God well, we need some work. However, even though we are far from perfect, God still wants to use us. As the body of Christ, we are God's hands and feet in the world. We are the way God acts in the world today.

Before we move on to the next (and final) section, there are a few other things we need to briefly touch on about this topic. So you know, there are two types of "church." There are "churches," and there is "the Church." *Little-c churches* are local groups made up of believers who work together for Christ. The *big-C Church* is the body/group of all believers everywhere. Little-c churches are a whole other topic, which needs its own book. Everything we have been discussing is about the big-C Church and what Christ is doing in the world today.

Also, we need to cover two phrases you have probably heard if you have spent much time in a church. Both of these are usually overcomplicated. However, there is a very simple (but important) meaning to them that relates to Christ as the head of the body, the Church.

The first is: *"Christ in you."* Very simply, this means Christ is working in the world today through Christians. The logic goes like this: The Church is the primary way Christ is working in the world. The Church is made up of people who follow Christ, i.e. *Christians.* That means Christ is working in and through Christians. So, if you're a Christian, then Christ is working in the world today *in* and *through you.* Saying Christ is *in you* is shorthand for saying Christ is working in the world in and through you.

The other phrase that is frequently overcomplicated is a lot like this one. It is: *"in Christ."* To be "in Christ" simply means to be "in the kingdom of Christ." It is the identification of the kingdom with its ruler. *"In Christ"* is just shorthand for "in the kingdom of Christ."

Essentially, to be in the kingdom of Christ just means you're playing on Christ's team. Like in a sporting event that has two teams playing, it just means you're playing on one team and not the other. You're on Christ's team rather than the other team. (We'll talk more about this in the next section).

So, let's pull everything together from this section. Here are the four main points we have covered:

1. <u>Image of Christ</u>—You represent Christ by who you are and what you do.

2. <u>Head of the body, the Church</u>—The Church is the way Christ is working in the world today.

3. <u>Christ in you</u>—Christ is working in the world today in and through you.

4. <u>In Christ</u>—You're playing on Christ's team instead of another team.

You might notice that these are all related. These are basically several different ways of describing the same thing. Humans were created to be Christ's representatives (images) on earth. This was and is our job. We don't always represent him very well, but it is still our job to represent him.

And that's it. That's the main point. We are to represent Christ. He is the head, and we are the body. We are to follow his lead and do as he would do in our situations. There are, however, obvious limitations. For example, we don't have anywhere near the power that he does. But in our limited capacity, we are to represent Christ and be his hands and feet in the world.

7. Reconciler of All Creation

Finally, we come to our last point: reconciler of all creation. This speaks to how Christ has changed the outcome of the story of God and man. There are two parts to the end of this story: 1) The End of the Battle and 2) The End of Humanity's Present Condition.

The End of the Battle

Here's what happened: In the beginning, Christ created the heavens and the earth. (He is the uncreated creator, after all). And when he created everything, it was good. God and man were in harmony.

At some point, something happened that theologians call "the

Fall." A big part of what happened at the Fall was that creation split into two kingdoms or teams: the kingdom of Christ and the domain of darkness. In the previous section, we talked about Christians playing for the team of Christ. Well, prior to the Fall, everyone played for the team of Christ.

With the Fall, everybody essentially left Christ's team and started playing for the other side. All of the players on Christ's team decided they would rather do things their own way instead of following Christ's lead (he was the captain, after all). So, they started playing for the other team, the domain of darkness. Even though creation split into two teams with the Fall, one day Christ will reconcile the two teams. But what does that mean?

The problem at this point is that we modern people only really know of one kind of reconciliation: people shaking hands, making up, and becoming friends again. In the New Testament world, the world of the Roman Empire, that was one possible meaning of *reconciliation*. But there was another one. Let's take a look at the historical background to the word *reconciliation*. It will help all this make more sense.

At the time of the New Testament, the Roman Empire controlled a vast area. They conquered many nations and not surprisingly, not all of those nations were happy to be living under Roman rule. From time to time, one or more of them would think about taking a shot at winning their independence from Rome in battle. Rome, with its many (and very good) armies, would basically say, "You sure about that?"

Now, there would be one of two ways this could go. Option 1 was for the rebelling nation to realize they messed up, willingly submit to Rome, agree to be its subjects again, and pay whatever penalties Rome imposed on them. Option 2 was for the rebelling nation to try and fight for their independence. If they chose option 1, things would return to normal, and there would be peace— as well as higher taxes or some other such penalty. If they chose option 2, they would fight Rome in battle, and they would lose, because Rome was really good at fighting. Rome would stomp their armies, take control, force everyone to submit to their rule, and then declare peace.

So, no matter which option the rebelling nation chose, the two nations would be reconciled and there would be peace—because *Roman peace* just meant the end of hostilities. It didn't mean the two parties got along; they often didn't. But no matter which option the rebelling nation chose, they would almost certainly end up serving Rome, because Rome pretty much always won its wars. The only real difference is the manner in which the rebelling nation would end up serving Rome. If they submitted willingly, things wouldn't be *too* bad. If Rome had to fight you to get you to submit, they were going to punish you.

This is the historical background to the word *reconciliation*. This is how people hearing Christians talk about reconciliation in the first century would have understood it.

Now, there is one big way Christ and Rome are similar, and there are a couple of big ways they are different. Let's start with how they are similar. Like reconciliation to Rome, Christ's reconciliation is going to happen either way. There's nothing you can do about it. Rebelling against Rome didn't work very well, because Rome was very powerful. And rebelling against Christ isn't going to work at all for the same reason. Think about it. Do you really think you can fight the uncreated creator? I mean, really?

In the end, the fighting will end, and there will be "peace" for everyone. The manner of that peace, though, will be different for different people—depending on whether they insist on continuing to rebel or not. Basically, you can either bow down or you can be put down. It's your choice, but you're not going to be able to continue to rebel. That just won't happen.

Now, that's the end of the similarities between Roman reconciliation and Christ's reconciliation. Let's talk about the differences. The biggest way Christ and Rome are different is how they treat people who are part of their kingdom/empire/team.

The Romans were often a bunch of jerks. They weren't necessarily very nice to the people they ruled, and while that was pretty standard for empires in the ancient world, it wasn't any fun for the people being ruled. It's not hard to understand why some people would want to try to rebel. Christ, on the other hand, sacrificed himself by dying on a cross (death by torture) so the people who join his team can become beautiful and completely flawless human beings. It's hard to imagine a bigger contrast.

Another way Christ and Rome are different is Christ doesn't penalize you for choosing the peaceful option. Rome would penalize you for even thinking about rebelling (by imposing even higher taxes on you than you're already paying or something like that). Christ is not trying to force you to follow him so you will pay your taxes. Christ is trying to renew you into being truly human once again. His ultimate goal is to help *you*. You are not a means to an end. You *are* the end.

OK, so all of that is interesting, but what does that mean for us? What happened to humans in the Fall, and how is Christ fixing it?

The End of Humanity's Present Condition

The reason humanity becoming somewhat broken creatures is called the "*Fall*" and is quite simply because humans fell. With the Fall, they took an unpleasant and harsh step "down." Humans were made in the image of God and reflected the divine in everything they did. But when they fell, they dropped down a bit.

The Fall is sort of like when you're walking along and not paying attention, but suddenly you discover that you've actually reached a downward staircase when your front foot falls and you stumble or slide down a few steps before you catch yourself. You don't fall all the way down the stairs, but you fall partway. You get an adrenaline rush, your body enters emergency mode, and you feel both off balance and a little scared about how bad that could have been. You're glad you didn't fall all the way down the stairs, but you're mentally kicking yourself for not noticing the stairs in the first place. *That*, right there, is the Fall.

Humans were walking along and not paying attention to the downward staircase in front of them. Then, they fell down a few stairs. Only in this case, these were no ordinary stairs. The top of the stairs is true humanity. The bottom of the stairs is complete loss of humanity. Humans fell partway down *those* stairs. Not good.

Christ is like a helpful person who happens to be standing on the stairs. He keeps us from falling all the way down and helps us catch our balance again. The thing is, again, these are no ordinary stairs. So, what happens next is a little different and a lot more important.

Christ has stabilized us, but we have a choice to make. Do we let him help us back up to the top, or do we decide we want to go our own way and continue heading down the stairs? At the top of the stairs lies true humanity. Everything we talked about in the sections on Firstborn from the Dead, Beginner of a New Humanity, and Head of the Body, the Church is at the top of the stairs. At the bottom, lies the opposite of these things—the complete loss of humanity. So, do we go up the stairs or down the stairs?

The answer *should* be obvious. We *should* let Christ help us back up to the top of the stairs. After all, that's where we become truly human. There, we become fully renewed in God's image and fully remade into the beautiful human beings we were always meant to be. However, while this decision is easy to make in a vacuum, it's much more difficult to make in real life.

The thing is though, we are not able to just stay in the middle of the staircase forever. We have to make a choice which way we are going to go. Because we are all mortal, at some point we will die. When that happens, we will finish going whichever direction we are headed. If we're headed up, we'll finish our upward journey with the next life. If we're headed down, we'll finish our downward journey with the next life. Everyone will either go up the stairs or down the stairs. The next two chapters will explain this further.

Conclusion

We have now worked through all of the main points about the person and work of Christ. These seven things explain who he is and what he has done, and they are the theological foundations for the Christian worldview. Let's briefly review them.

1. Image of the Invisible God

   Images represent someone or something else. Christ as the image of the invisible God means that if you want to know what God looks like, you need to look at Christ. And because he is a person, Christ doesn't just reflect God. Christ represents God.

2. Uncreated Creator

   Christ created everything that was created in all of existence. However, he himself is uncreated. He is creat-*or* rather than creat-*ion*.

3. Temple of God

   First, this is where man meets God. God is everywhere, but He dwells in Christ in a special way—just like He did with the Temple. Also, because of Christ's sacrifice, sinful man is able to approach the holy God. Second, this is where God meets man. The divine and the human come together in a single person, Jesus of Nazareth.

4. Firstborn from the Dead

   Jesus was the first person to pass through death and come

out the other side—never to die again. His death and res-
urrection is what allows sinful man to approach the holy
God (Temple of God). His resurrection also gives us hope.
Our future is now different because of what he has done.

5. <u>Beginner of a New Humanity</u>

Everybody is beautiful and everybody is broken. Christ's
resurrection matters because it fixes our broken parts and
makes our beautiful parts shine even more brightly. We
were made to reflect and represent God. Christ is re-mak-
ing us into people who are truly human.

6. <u>Head of the Body, the Church</u>

Humans were created to be God's representatives on
Earth—His images. We don't always represent God well,
but that's our job. The primary way Christ acts in the world
today is through us. He is the head, and we are the body.

7. <u>Reconciler of All Creation</u>

The battle between good and evil will end one day. However, while the end of the war is certain, our individual
battles continue. We have two options. We can either let
Christ remake us into people who reflect and represent
God. Or, we can choose to go our own way and lose what
humanity we have left.

These are the main points of theology for the Christian worldview. In the previous chapter, we took a look at the first link in
the chain: the truth of Christianity. There, we saw there is good
reason to think Christianity is actually true. But we were left
with the question: "What is Christianity?"

In this chapter, we looked at the theology of the Christian worldview. This painted a picture of what the world looks like from a Christian perspective. How we live our lives is going to be based on what we talked about in this chapter, because everything is based on who Christ is and what he has done.

But even though how we live our lives is based on who Christ is and what he has done, we haven't really touched on what our daily lives should look like. And we haven't touched on how living a "Christian" life works. We might ask questions like: "Why does God tell us to live in a particular way?", "How does following God's commands actually lead to renewal?", and "How does what we do in this life affect what we do in the next life?"

In the next chapter, Beliefs and Actions, we're going to talk about a lot of these How? questions—you know, how all of this stuff actually works. Then, in the chapter after that, we're going to talk about what the Christian life actually looks like.

CHAPTER 4

Beliefs and Actions (Link 3)

Introduction

This chapter fills a gap for most of us. We know what theology is. Even if we don't know much about theology, we know what it is. And we know God wants people to live in a certain way. Whether we believe in God or not, we understand the idea that if there is a God, then He would probably want people to do some things and not do others. But we're a little fuzzy on how the two connect. "Why does God care what we do?", "Why does God command these particular actions?", and "Why would we want to follow God's commands anyway?"

This chapter answers these sorts of questions. It is the third link in the Christian worldview. And like links in a chain, all of them are connected and all of them have to be strong for the whole thing to work.

We started with the truth of Christianity (link 1). Then, we looked at the person and work of Christ (link 2). The final link will be the Christian life (link 4). This chapter explains how link 2 and link 4 connect. It explains how theology and all that stuff about Jesus we talked about in the last chapter actually connects with our everyday lives.

As you are reading this chapter and thinking through these

questions, you will really want to focus on section 3, The Spiral. The spiral is the single most important thing in this chapter. It explains how renewal into the image of God works in our daily lives, and it is how beliefs and actions (or theology and practice) connect. If you get nothing else from this chapter, make sure you understand the spiral (section 3).

1. <u>The Beginning</u>—God's Commands Are Based on Who He Is
God seems to make a lot of demands on humans: "Do this!" and "Don't do that!" And most of the time, we have no idea why He's telling us to do or to not do something. He just tells us to obey. Of course, if God actually exists, it does kind of make sense to obey Him. He is God after all. But it sure would be nice to have an answer to what seems to be a really simple (and reasonable) question: "Why?" Basically, we want to ask God: "Why are we supposed to act in this particular way? Other ways are more fun or more easy. Why do you, God, always seem to want us to do things the hard way?"

The answer actually takes us back to something we discussed in the last chapter: the image of God. We talked about how Christ is the image of the invisible God. Christ represents God by his actions, and when he does something, he is acting on God's behalf. Christ's actions reflect *who God is*.

Similarly, we humans were made in the image of God. We were also created to represent God and act on His behalf. We don't always do that very well, but that's our job. So, in order to represent God well, we have to actually act the way He would act. Our actions need to reflect *who God is*.

That means that in order to reflect God, we need to actually act like God. That means our actions need to reflect *who God is*. That's why God commands us to do the things He commands us to do. We need to be good reflections of Him; we need to look like Him. Because of that, God bases His commands to us on *who He is*—so that we reflect and represent Him accurately.

REVELATION AND RENEWAL • 73

However, even though we are all reflecting God, we are not supposed to be exact copies of one another. We are all commanded to be like God and do what He would do. However, each of us does that in our own unique way. *Should* we love others? Yes. *How* do we put that into practice? That's up to each one of us, and we all do it a little differently.

2. The Direction—Following God's Commands Helps Us Know God Himself

I know it sounds a little odd to say following God's commands helps us to know God Himself. But think back to what we talked about in the last section: God's commands are based on who He is. If that's true, then the idea that following God's commands will help us know God Himself may not be so crazy after all. Let's talk about that some more.

If God's commands are based on who He is, then the reason God tells us to love others is because God is loving. The reason God tells us to care for the poor is because God cares for the poor. Because God's commands are based on who He is, they give us a window into His character. We know something about *who* God is based on what He commands.

What all of that means is that when we practice the way of life God commands, we *experience* His character. When we love others, we experience firsthand the love God has for others. When we care for the poor, we experience firsthand the concern God has for the poor. We get to know God by living like Him.

Another way we get to know God is actually similar to how we get to know people. The more we spend time with a person and interact with them, the better we get to know them. This works for all types of relationships: human and divine. It doesn't matter whether the person is a coworker, friend, family member, spouse, or God. As time progresses and we interact more and more, we get to know the other person better. That's just how relationships work. So, just like we get to know other humans better as we interact with them, we get to know God better as we interact with Him.

This relational knowledge is intensified by the fact that we are not merely hanging out with God. We are actively trying to accomplish something. Think back to the last chapter where we saw that Christ is the "head of the body, the Church." Christ is working to accomplish something in this world, and we are working with him. We are working with God through Christ to achieve an objective. You get to know someone much better and much faster when you're trying to achieve something with them.

Now, all of this relationship stuff is a bit different with God, because one of the parties in the relationship is God instead of a human. But the basic principles are the same. The more you spend time with someone, the better you get to know them. And actively working with someone on something causes you to get to know them much faster and in much greater depth than just passively spending time with them. Actively following God and working on a task together helps us get to know Him much better than we could if we just read about Him or talked about Him. *Doing* does more.

So, following God's commands and working on an objective with Him helps us to know Him better. But how does knowing God better and doing all the stuff God tells us to do actually *change* us? God is supposed to be renewing us through Christ, right?

At most, obeying God's commands sounds like we're forming good habits, and while that is good, it doesn't seem that impressive. Knowing God is impressive. But how does following God's commands help us move towards renewal? In order to answer that question, we need to talk about something called "the spiral." Pay attention to this next section, because it's really important.

3. The Spiral—Combining Beliefs and Actions Causes Change in Humans

Imagine a gymnast trying to do some complicated, new flippy-do (obviously, the technical term). How might he or she go about it? If the gymnast has a coach, very possibly it would start with the coach explaining how the flippy-do is supposed to work. Then, the gymnast gives it a try, or maybe several tries. Afterwards, the coach might say something like, "You have the first part right, but try doing the second part a little more like this."

Then, the gymnast goes back and tries again. The flippy-do looks a little better this time than it did last time. The coach gives some more help, the flippy-do looks even better, and this process continues on and on. Hopefully, it results in the gymnast mastering that particular flippy-do.

Do you see what is going on here? There is an interaction between theory and practice in which each part helps the other. Everything starts with theory: "This is how you do the motion. This is how the physics work." After the physics is explained, the gymnast gives it a try, which is *practice*. Practicing it actually helps with the theory, because trying something out helps the gymnast understand the theory better. It helps the gymnast understand the physics of the flippy-do.

Trying something helps take it from external to internal. Practice helps the gymnast understand the physics behind the motion. It doesn't change the physics, but it gives the gymnast a first-person perspective. Then, when the coach explains the theory again, it will make more sense, because the gymnast understands the motion better as a result of practicing it.

This interaction is not limited to complicated motions in sports. It is something that works in a lot of places, because it is simply about how theory and practice work together. And one of the places it works is in how we come to know God Himself better and how we start to look more like Him. The only difference here is that we're not talking about physics (theory) and trying to perform a complicated gymnastic motion (practice). We're talking about understanding God's will (theory) and living in a truly human way (practice).

What we have been talking about kind of sounds like we're going around and around in a circle. It sounds like something that looks like this:

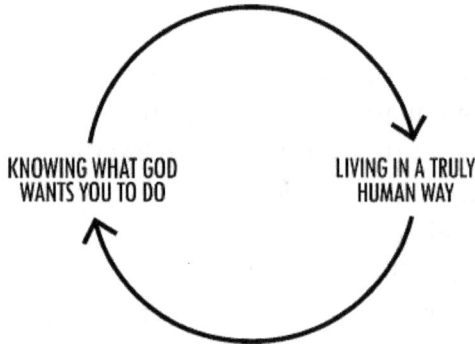

KNOWING WHAT GOD WANTS YOU TO DO

LIVING IN A TRULY HUMAN WAY

In reality though, we're not going around in a circle. If this were a circle, we would end up in the same place we started. Instead, we're moving on something that looks more like a spiral, because we end up in a higher place than we began.

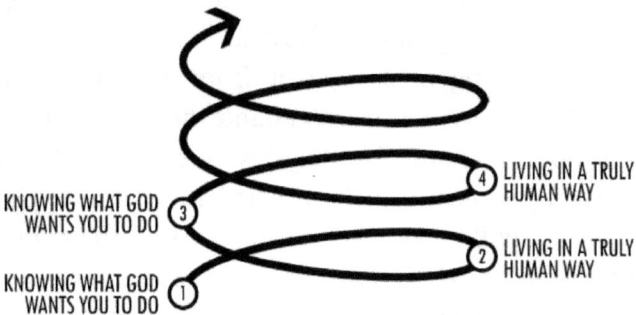

KNOWING WHAT GOD WANTS YOU TO DO ③

KNOWING WHAT GOD WANTS YOU TO DO ①

LIVING IN A TRULY HUMAN WAY ④

LIVING IN A TRULY HUMAN WAY ②

The spiral begins by knowing something about what God wants us to do. He reveals it to us. Now we have a choice: Do we act on it or not? If we act on it, then we learn and grow and become better people. We act in a more truly human way. As a result, we will understand what God is telling us to do *better* the next time around.

Remember how the gymnast understood the theory better after practicing the motion? The same works here. After we practice living out what we know about how God wants us to live, we come to a greater and deeper understanding of who God is and what He wants for us. We are now back to the point at which we started (the theory side of things)—only this time, we are a little higher up. That is why I call this the spiral.

4. <u>The Goal</u>—We Are Being Renewed into the Image of God
The spiraling up process we just talked about *is* the renewal process. This is what it looks like on a day-to-day basis to be renewed in the image of God. God lets us know what He wants us to do, and we try living it out in the best way we can. We make mistakes, certainly, but practicing living a godly life helps us understand God better the next time He tells us what He wants us to do. Each part helps the other.

At this point, there are two questions I think we need to answer. First, "Where is the spiral headed?" and second, "What does the end of the spiral look like?" Truthfully, we have already talked about the answer to both of these questions, even though I didn't explain it at the time. Let's look at that now.

Think back to the first two sections in this chapter. In the first section, we saw that God's commands are based on who He is. That means when God tells us to do something, His commands are based directly on His character: who He is. In the second section, we saw that following God's commands helps us to know God Himself. Since the commands He gives us are based on who He is, then by following those commands, we get to know God Himself. So, the answer to the question, "Where is the spiral headed?" is: knowledge of God Himself. The full spiral diagram looks like this:

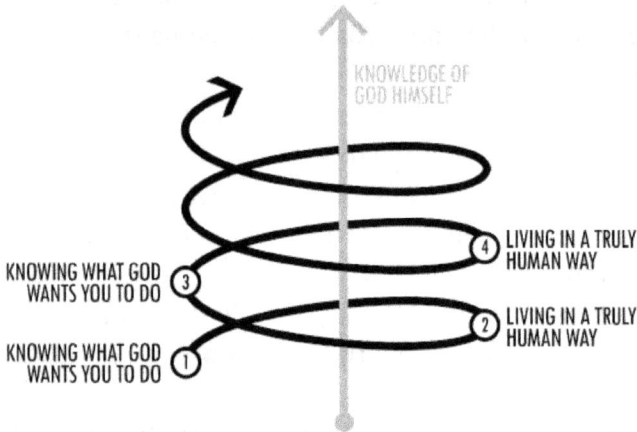

KNOWLEDGE OF GOD HIMSELF

KNOWING WHAT GOD WANTS YOU TO DO ③

KNOWING WHAT GOD WANTS YOU TO DO ①

④ LIVING IN A TRULY HUMAN WAY

② LIVING IN A TRULY HUMAN WAY

Now, let's look at the second question: "What does the end of the spiral look like?" Because this spiral describes our renewal process, the first thing we should know is that it is not going to be completed in this life. We won't reach the end now. The spiral begins in this life, and it will be completed with the next life.

As far as what the end of the upward spiral looks like, we actually have already discussed that, too. The upward spiral describes our renewal into the image of God. Now, because images reflect someone or something else, that means when we are completely renewed, we will reflect God. When people look at us, they will see God.

Additionally, because we are people and not objects (like statues, faces on coins, or pictures on our phones), the way we are images is different. We don't just reflect God. We represent God. We are His hands and feet in the world—the way He acts in the world. This is what it means for humans to live as images of God, and this is what humans were always meant to be. *Full renewal,* then, is living as full and complete humans. We will be the reflections and representatives of God that we were always meant to be.

Unfortunately, this spiral is not upwards only. There is also a downward spiral. If we know God wants us to do something and we choose to ignore Him or act in the opposite way to what He wants, we begin our path downward. We reject the opportunity to live correctly and improve our actions. That means we reject our knowledge of who God is and what He wants us to do.

By doing this, we would be like a gymnast who refuses to practice what their coach tells them and instead sits around doing nothing. Or worse, we might practice the wrong things and build bad habits. Additionally, as a result of ignoring or actively disobeying the coach, the relationship between gymnast and coach begins to break down. At best, the gymnast will not become as good as he or she could have been. At worst, his or her future as a gymnast may come to an end.

The same thing is true for us and our relationship with God. If we ignore God, we reject the knowledge He has given us about who He is and what He wants us to do. And if we refuse to practice what we have been taught, the relationship between our coach (God) and us begins to break down.

Now, God is patient. He has and will put up with a lot from us. But His patience only lasts for so long. At some point, it will become clear that we have no interest in the renewal He wants for us. God's patience will run out, and He will stop trying to help us. At that point, our future as humans will come to an end.

The end of the upward spiral is renewal into true humanity. We will become humans as humans were always meant to be. The end result of the downward spiral is the loss of our humanity. We will become ex-humans.

Before finishing this section, I need to make one final point. There really is no such thing as staying steady in one place on the spiral. We are either going up or we are going down. There is no way to avoid this. God *is* going to reveal things to us. He *is* going to tell us about Himself and how we should live as humans. Our coach *is* going to tell us how to do the motions. There is no stopping that. The only thing we have any control over is how we respond to what we are told.

Furthermore, when God lets us know we are going down a wrong path or that there is a right path we need to start down, we *will* respond. We will respond whether we want to or not, because even ignoring God is still a response. Isn't the gymnast ignoring the coach still responding to the coach? Ignoring the coach *is* a response—and not a very nice one at that. Isn't ignoring God still responding to God—and doing it in a not very nice way?

God is going to reach out to us, and there's nothing we can do to stop that. But we really shouldn't *want* to stop God reaching out to us. Remember, "everybody is beautiful, and everybody is broken"? Well, the second part of that is that we're all broken. We need to be fixed, and we need God to fix us. He is reaching out to us because He cares about us and we need help. There is nothing a loving God can do but to reach out to His creations when they are in trouble.

Furthermore, the first part of that statement is "everybody is beautiful." We should want to be the most beautiful humans we can be. Just as God is reaching out to us because we are in trouble, God is also trying to help us to be the best versions of ourselves.

In the end, the only question that really matters for us is: "Will we respond well to God and spiral up, or will we respond poorly and spiral down?" Will we take the path upward toward renewal into true humans, or will we take the path downward toward losing our humanity and becoming ex-humans?

5. The Focus—We Should Prepare for Life with God

Death is not the end, nor is it the beginning. It is the point of transition from this part of our existence to the next.

Christians often talk about *where* a person goes after this life. This is a mistake. The New Testament rarely speaks of the *place* of the afterlife, because frankly, it's not that important. The next life is not about a place; it's about a person. It's about going to be with God in person.

In fact, we probably should not think of the next life as wildly different from this life. Oh, there will be many things that will be different. Life with God will be without pain, without sorrow, and without all the negative things from this life. The bad will be gone, and the good will be increased beyond anything we can imagine. But that is only a difference of degree (though, it will be a large difference). However, it is not a difference in essence or nature.

You see, what happens is that what we begin here in this life will be taken to its conclusion, its completion, with the next life. Think about the spiral. All of us are either spiraling up or spiraling down. When we transition to the next life, our spirals will be completed. If we are heading up, we will finish our journey all the way up. If we are headed down, we will finish our journey all the way down.

Have you ever seen someone make enormous changes in their life—either good or bad? I'm talking about someone who has either made good decisions and completely pulled their life together and gotten out of a bad place, or someone who was in a good place but has made bad decisions and completely lost everything. Well, think about that multiplied a million times. That sort of change (for better or worse) is what will happen to us. When we transition to the next life, our spiral up or down will be completed. We will either finish our renewal process and become truly human, or we will finish our rejection of the image of God and become ex-humans.

The wise thing to do is to prepare for our future. If Christianity is true and our future is focused on, shaped by, and centered around our connection with God, then we should prepare for that now. We should prioritize whatever puts us on the right path with God and give everything else a lower level of importance.

So, are we having a nice life, or are we spiraling up? Are we enjoying the daily routines we have set up for ourselves, or are we becoming more truly human? These things don't *have* to be opposed to each other, but they often are. Having a nice life is fine *only as long as* your real goal is spiraling up, becoming more truly human, and knowing God Himself.

The problem is that we can really only aim at one thing. If we aim at a nice life, we will almost certainly miss God. If we aim at God, we will almost certainly miss a nice life. Now, it is absolutely possible that God wants us to have a nice life. But remember Jesus told people, "Take up your cross and follow me." And remember, a cross was a method of death by torture. That kind of lets us know what Jesus thought about a nice life. Besides, if you aim at God and actually hit your target, you won't really care about a "nice" life anyway. God is better.

Now, none of this is easy to hear. But wouldn't you rather know what's true? No one wants to hear they have to choose between pursuing a nice life and pursuing a relationship with God. But wouldn't you rather hear the truth than something that sounds good but ultimately takes you somewhere bad?

Perhaps after seeing all of this, it makes more sense why Jesus said: "Blessed are the poor in spirit," "blessed are those who mourn," "blessed are those who hunger and thirst for righteousness," and "blessed are the pure in heart" (Matthew 5). Temporary happiness is not as important as knowing God. And if our next life is the completion of what we begin in this life, then we should focus on the long term rather than the short term. We should live for where we're headed. We should aim for God.

6. The Fallout—The Christian Path Has Consequences

Following the Christian path, quite simply, is not normal. It is not normal to prioritize your next life at the expense of this life. It is not normal to care more about your relationship with God than having a nice, comfortable, or fun life. Doing these things makes you weird.

Of course, that is sort of the point. We're supposed to look like Christ. We're not supposed to look like everyone else, because Christ didn't look like everyone else. The whole point of reflecting and representing God is to actually reflect and represent God—like Christ did. That means we are going to look and act differently than everyone around us. The problem is: not everyone will like that.

If you stand up for something, there will be some who would prefer you sit back down. That's just how people work. Lots of people didn't like Jesus either, and they would have preferred he sat back down. He didn't, and as a result, his life didn't go too well by earthly standards. If we reflect and represent God, we shouldn't be surprised if the same happens to us.

Here's why this happens. Certain things in this world are actually true. That means some of our beliefs will be inflexible, because the truth is not flexible. Some people won't like that. Furthermore, because beliefs and actions are connected, our actions are not separate from our beliefs. So, if some of our beliefs are inflexible, some of our actions are going to be inflexible as well. Some people *really* won't like that.

Reality check: Being inflexible does NOT mean you are obnoxious to those around you. You don't get to be a jerk, slap a Jesus label on what you do, and then claim persecution when people don't like you. They don't like you because you're a jerk. It's not because you look like Jesus. You only get to claim persecution when: 1) You are actually doing what Jesus would do, and 2) The negative reaction people give you is actually something serious.

Let me say it again just to be clear. Being inflexible on certain beliefs and actions does not mean you get to be a jerk, claim you're following Jesus, and feel like you're doing the right thing. NO. Being inflexible on certain beliefs and actions is only OK when you're *actually* following God and *actually* doing the right thing. Everything here depends on whether you're actually doing the right thing or not. And that's why it's so important to know what is actually true. You cannot take a stand for truth if you don't know what the truth is.

The point of all this is that if you stand up for something, some people will not like that you have taken a stand. It is good to be diplomatic, and you should try to be at peace with everyone as much as possible. But no matter how diplomatic you are, there will be consequences—even if you don't want them. If you represent Christ, the people who don't follow Christ won't like you. After all, they are playing for the other team and working against you.

Let me make one final point, and I don't want you to miss this. The true followers of Christ are not always the people we think they are. Jesus cuts across categories. The truth often does that. Many times the people we think are furthest from the truth are actually the closest. And many of the people we think are the closest to the truth are actually the furthest away. Jesus told his own disciples (Matthew 13:24–30) not to try to sort out who was who, because they would get it wrong. Do you know better?

We may think we know who is and who isn't following God, but it will often be unclear who the true followers are until everything is revealed. And when everything is finally revealed, there will be surprises.

7. <u>The Reason</u>—Thankfulness Is Why We Want to Follow This Path

It can easily seem like being thankful is just one of those "nice Christian things" that doesn't mean very much. However, thankfulness (or thanksgiving) actually plays an important role in the life of the Christian. Thankfulness is what keeps us going *up* the spiral.

The spiral begins when God tells us something that He wants us to do. At that point, we can either choose to do what God has told us to do, or we can reject or ignore it. The reason we *want* to obey God is because we are thankful for everything He has done for us. In the chapter on the person and work of Christ, we talked a lot about what He has done for us through Christ. Remember how Christ went through death by torture and then rose from the dead? That wasn't because he thought it would be fun. *We* needed him to do that—so he could fix *us*. So, maybe we should be at least a little thankful.

It is actually a good idea to follow God anyway. God does know more than us, after all. So, the wise thing for us to do would be to listen to Him. But we're talking about something more than that. The fact that God knows more than us explains why we *should* follow God: because it makes sense. Thankfulness explains why we would *want* to follow God: because we are thankful for everything He has done for us.

Ultimately, we should want our spiral to move upwards. That's where true humanity and knowledge of God Himself are. The only way that won't happen, though, is if the spiral fails at one of its two points. Either: 1) God stops revealing things to us and telling us what He wants us to do, or 2) We stop acting on that knowledge and following God's will. I wouldn't plan on God not holding up His end, so really it comes down to us. Will we hold up our end? Will we do what God tells us to do?

Thankfulness is what makes us want to hold up our end. It is what keeps the spiral moving upwards. The only place the upward spiral can fail is on our end, and thankfulness is what makes us *want* to do the right thing.

In our brief discussion of thankfulness, we have actually answered a question many of us have but may never have gotten a good answer to. "Why would I *want* to live like God tells me to?" Or we could phrase the question like: "Why would I *want* to live a moral life?" The answer is: "Because of everything God has done for us."

Again, it makes good sense to follow God, because He is actually God. That should be reason enough. But we should *want* to follow God, because of everything He has done for us. He is renewing us into true humans—something that cost Christ personally to achieve. And in this whole process, God is being patient with us ignoring Him and outright rejecting Him. He is doing that because He cares for us and wants the best for us. Thankfulness for both His sacrifice and His patience is the only appropriate response.

Conclusion

We covered seven points in this chapter about how beliefs (theory) and actions (practice) interact. These answer a lot of the "How?" and "Why?" questions we often have about Christianity. Here they are:

1. The Beginning—God's Commands Are Based on Who He Is

   Our job is to reflect and represent God. Our actions tell people who He is. Therefore, God bases His commands to us on who He is so that we will reflect and represent Him well.

2. The Direction—Following God's Commands Helps Us Know God Himself

   Because God's commands are based on who He is, doing what God commands lets us experience His character firsthand. We get to know God by following Him and actively working on something together.

3. The Spiral—Combining Beliefs and Actions Causes Change in Humans

   Everything starts with revelation from God (theory). God reveals something to us or commands us to do something.

We then try to live out what God tells us to do (practice). This practice helps us understand the theory better. As a result, we are in a higher place when we get more theory. We have moved upward.

4. The Goal—We Are Being Renewed into the Image of God

The upward spiral is headed to knowledge of God Himself. It results in our renewal into the image of God and the restoration of our humanity. The end of the downward spiral is rejection of the image of God and the loss of our humanity.

5. The Focus—We Should Prepare for Life with God

Christianity says that the afterlife is about God and the way in which we relate to Him. If that's true, then we should prepare for that now. We should focus more on spiraling up than on having a comfortable life.

6. The Fallout—The Christian Path Has Consequences

If you stand up for something, some people will try to make you sit back down. This is to be expected. Learn the truth and stand up for it—regardless of the consequences. But remain open to correction. Nobody is perfect.

7. The Reason—Thankfulness Is Why We Want to Follow This Path

God has done a lot for us. Recognizing what He has done and being thankful for it makes us want to follow Him. Thankfulness is what keeps the spiral moving upward.

If you take nothing else away from this chapter, you should make sure to remember the spiral. It explains *how* beliefs and actions connect. It is the glue that holds theology and practice together. And it explains *how* renewal actually works in our daily lives.

To briefly review the spiral, let's go back to the gymnast. The coach tells the gymnast how to do a motion (theory). Then, the gymnast tries the motion out in real life (practice). And once the gymnast has tried the motion in the real world (practice), when he or she talks to the coach again, the coach's instruction (theory) will make more sense. Trying something in real life helps you understand the theory better so that you'll have a higher level of understanding the next time you try the thing again.

The same thing happens with God (the coach) and humans (the gymnast). God lets us know something about Himself or something we should do in our lives. Then, if we practice what God has told us, we will understand what He has said in a deeper way. And the next time He goes over the thing with us, we will understand it even better. As a result, the second time we try to put something into practice, we will be better at it than the first time.

This is what a correct interaction between God and humans looks like. God is going to tell us what He wants, and if we are doing life correctly, we will try to live it out the best we can. We will get some parts right, and we will mess up other parts. But by trying it out, we see where our mistakes are and get a deeper understanding of the parts we already understood.

Then, when God tells us something again, we won't be starting at ground zero. We will be starting up a step. And each time we go through this process, if we try to do what God is telling us to do, we will take a step up. This continual upwards motion as we go back and forth between God telling us stuff (theory) and us trying to live it out (practice) is the *upward spiral.*

So, how does this fit into the big picture? When we were

talking about theology, we saw that as a result of the Fall, the world was divided into two camps, kingdoms, or teams. In the first one, people are separated from God and do whatever they want. While doing whatever you want sounds nice, it may not be quite as nice once you look beneath the surface. If what we learned about the image of God is correct, and if true humanity can only be found by reflecting and representing God, then the people who go their own way and ignore God are missing out on full and true humanity.

On the other hand, if reflecting and representing God is what true humanity really is all about, then if we want to be truly human, we need to pursue reflecting and representing God. And that is why the *spiral* is so important. It is the process by which we move toward true humanity in this life. It is how God is beginning to fix all of our broken parts and to make the beautiful parts shine even more brightly.

However, becoming more truly human is not just about becoming better people all by ourselves. The sort of person we are affects the world around us. A good person will make a positive impact on the world around them. A bad person will make a negative impact on the world around them. The better we are, the more of a positive effect we will have on the world around us.

In the last chapter, we talked about what it means for Christ to be *"in us."* It means Christ is working in the world through us. By becoming truly human ourselves, the small part of the world that we occupy becomes better. And because what we do affects others, by becoming better humans ourselves, we make a positive impact on the world around us.

That is why it is so important to live the life Christ wants us to live. It's not just about us; it's about the people and the world around us. When we tell people that we are Christians, we are showing ourselves off as the works of Christ. Like living paintings, we show what the painter can do. And we don't just need to look good on the surface. We need to actually *be* good, because people can tell the difference. And if we're not *actually* good; if we don't live a *truly* Christian life, we won't represent Christ well.

But what does it mean to live a Christian life? Do we go to church a lot and invite our friends to go with us? Do we try to be nice to everyone we meet and show them "love"? The answer is both simple and not simple. It is simple in that it is not complicated. But it is not simple in that it is hard to do, and it takes both strength and courage to apply yourself to it fully. The next chapter is focused on exactly what the Christian life looks like.

CHAPTER 5

The Christian Life (Link 4)

Introduction

We all know what the Christian life is, right? You're supposed to go to church, read the Bible, pray, and generally try to do what Jesus would do (even though we're not entirely sure what that last one means). Well, those are all certainly good things. But *why* do we do things like that? What exactly are we trying to accomplish?

Even if we go to church several times a week, there are still quite a few hours left in the week. What are we supposed to do with those hours? We can read the Bible and pray for some of that time, but what do we do when we go to work or school, hang out with our friends, or do any number of the other things we do in a normal life? How are we supposed to act during that time?

All that Christian stuff is meant to *do* something. You don't go to church because God is taking attendance. You don't read the Bible or pray in order to build up hours because God is keeping count. There has to be a reason. So, what is the Christian life, really?

This is the final link in our series of four links that is the Christian worldview. And remember, like a chain, each link has to be strong for the chain itself to be strong. If Christianity isn't true (link 1), then none of the things it says about who Christ is and what he has done matter (link 2). But if Christ hasn't actually done anything to help us (link 2), then there is no process of becoming a better human (link 3). And if there is no process of becoming a better human (link 3), then there is no actual "Christian life" that we're trying to become better at (link 4).

So, don't think of the Christian life as something that's just out there all on its own that we're just supposed to do because that's how we were raised (if you grew up in church, that is). Think of the Christian life as the natural result of everything we have been discussing for the last three chapters. If Christianity is true (link 1), if Jesus is who Christianity says he is and has actually made a way for us to be more truly human (link 2), and if there is a way to *become* truly human (link 3), then the Christian life matters (link 4).

1. Receive Revelation and Renewal

The first step in the Christian life is receiving revelation and renewal. Essentially, *revelation* is God telling us stuff about Himself, letting us know how to interact with Him, and explaining how we can live truly human lives. *Renewal* is renewal into the image of God. It happens by spiraling up, and it results in us becoming truly human. Revelation is the direction; renewal is getting to our destination. So, how do we receive revelation and renewal? What does that even mean?

This section will have three parts: 1) Finding Revelation, 2) Receiving Revelation, and 3) Receiving Renewal. If you're wondering why we're not talking about "finding renewal," it's because renewal isn't something we find. Renewal happens by responding correctly to revelation. That's what the spiral is all about. Let's just start with finding revelation, and I think you'll understand what's going on as we begin to move forward.

Finding Revelation

When we talked about the spiral, we saw that it began with God revealing something about Himself to us. That means He either shares some sort of knowledge with us or He tells us something He wants us to do. Then, we saw that we have the responsibility to act on that knowledge.

Now, God certainly does reveal things to individuals about their unique paths in life. But not everything that God has revealed comes directly to us as individuals. There are other ways God has revealed Himself as well. In this section, we are going to talk about three of the ways God reveals Himself and His will to us (though, there are others).

The first way God reveals Himself is through His creation. We talked about this in the chapter, The Truth of Christianity. Essentially, we can know something about who God is by looking at the world He has made. The upside to this is we get to see God actually at work in creation. This helps us get a sort of big picture view of God that keeps us from putting Him into a small little box like we sometimes do. The more we focus on our own problems and needs, the less we remember how large the universe is and how much God has created. The downside to looking at creation is that while we can learn some basics about God from the world around us, the picture we see is a little fuzzy. It's hard to get much clarity about God's character from creation.

Second, most of us have a gut feeling about what is right and wrong. Whether you call this a "conscience," "the internal witness of the Holy Spirit," or something else, we all have a sense about what things are right and what things aren't. This, I think, is something God has put in each one of us to help us make our way through this world.

The upside to this "gut feeling about right and wrong" is that it applies to our individual situations. It's not like a general command that you have to figure out how to apply to your situation. This is actually about *your* situation. The downside is that like our ability to know God from creation, our gut feeling about right and wrong is a little fuzzy. Because each one of us is not only beautiful but broken as well, our gut can be a little off. It is usually right, but because we are all a little broken, and have been raised and taught by people who are a little broken themselves, our gut moral feeling isn't right 100% of the time. As we become better humans, our gut becomes better at letting us know what is actually right and wrong, but it will never be perfect. Still, it's better to listen to what it says rather than ignore it. And our gut is pretty much always right when it tells us to do something we don't want to do (like forgive someone or be kind to someone).

Third, and finally, there is the Bible. Basically, this is the story of God's interaction with humanity. There is a lot in the Bible that lets us know what God is like, though some of it is not easy to understand. Most importantly, we have the life of Christ that tells us what it was like when God became human and lived among us. Those who were around Christ got to see the image of the invisible God in action and witness how God would respond to real-life situations. Then, they wrote about it so we could know what Christ was like as well.

The upside to this is that we can get some clear answers to some of our more specific questions that creation and our gut feeling just cannot address. The downside is that it takes work to figure out those answers. The basic message of the Gospels, the rest of the New Testament, and the whole Bible is not too hard to understand. But figuring out answers to specific questions can be difficult—especially when the culture we live in is different from that of the Bible.

Certainly, there are other sources of God's revelation. There are specific messages that the Holy Spirit gives individuals. And God often speaks to us through friends and wise individuals. Also, many would look to church tradition. To what extent God reveals Himself through any of these as well as how to understand them goes beyond the scope of this book.

What I want to do is talk about the role of revelation in the life of the Christian. What do we do with revelation once it has been given? And how does it make a difference in our daily lives? The three sources I listed above should be enough to accomplish that. They will get you thinking about how to: 1) See God in the world around you, 2) Experience God talking to you individually, and 3) Search for answers in the commands that God has given to all of us.

Again, the focus in this section is on receiving revelation and renewal. But since I'm talking about revelation, I wanted to give you an idea of what I meant by the word *revelation*, and point you toward the primary sources of God's revelation. The question is now: "What do we do with revelation once we have it?"

Receiving Revelation
The Christian life begins with receiving revelation. So, if we want the best possible Christian life we can have, if we want to know God Himself as well as we possibly can, we should start by receiving as much revelation as we can. Very simply, that means when God is talking to you, you pay attention.

As we discussed before, the spiral begins with God's revelation. In some ways, God reveals Himself to us, and we have no ability to stop that revelation—such as when we have a gut feeling that we are doing something wrong. In other ways, God's revelation just sits there waiting for us to pay attention. Scripture is a gold mine of revelation about God just waiting for us to dig into. We get to choose how much we want to learn and explore. God's work in creation lies somewhere between the two. Some of it we can't ignore, but there is much that we are unaware of until we actually take the time to look at it.

We are going to be presented with at least some level of God's revelation. The only question is, "What are we going to do with that revelation?" or "How are we going to respond?" In the section on the spiral, we saw that ignoring God is like ignoring our coach. If we ignore our coach, we are not going to progress as far as we could otherwise, and each time we ignore him, we damage the relationship. Any time God speaks to us, we should pay attention. Any revelation God has left for us to find, we should dig into.

Receiving Renewal

Receiving renewal is about acting on the revelation that we have received. If God tells us that we're not being kind to someone and we should be, then we should act on the knowledge that we have received. We should apologize for being mean and start being kind. If we're listening to a message on how to be a better person, we shouldn't spend our time thinking about how much so-and-so needs to hear this message. Instead, we should ask the question: "What do *I* need to hear in this message? What can *I* do to become a better person?"

Renewal doesn't come out of nowhere. It is based on the revelation we received from God. Revelation is like figuring out which way we should walk. Renewal is what happens when we actually start moving in that direction.

The Christian life does NOT start by fixing someone else. It starts by becoming fixed ourselves. We must become changed before we can change the world. Changing the world is good, and we'll get to that. But broken people are going to change the world in wrong ways. Change is only good if it's positive change. To make sure we're going to change the world for the better, we need to become better people ourselves.

Jesus is often quoted as saying, "Don't judge others." This comes from Matthew 7:1. However, if you read the next few verses, what you'll find is that this is not a command not to judge; rather, it is a command not to be a hypocrite. In other words, before you try to help someone with their problem, make sure you're not guilty of the same thing. Jesus says to get your own problem fixed, because only then will you be truly capable of helping someone else with their problem. If you want to change the world, become changed yourself first.

The thing is, we actually are supposed to change the world. In the chapter on theology, we saw that the Church is the body of Christ. We are the way Christ is working in the world today. We *are* supposed to change the world. But before we can do that, we have to become changed ourselves. We need to first *receive* revelation and renewal, and only then can we *share* revelation and renewal. We cannot share what we have not received. We will spend most of this chapter discussing concrete ways to receive revelation and renewal. Then, in the last section, we will talk about what it means to share revelation and renewal.

2. Stop Acting Selfishly

When we were looking at theology, we saw that in the beginning, everything was created good. But at some point, creation fell and everything got messed up. The world split into two teams: the kingdom of Christ and the domain of darkness. Everyone who was on God's team suddenly moved to the other team. People started fighting against their creator. We decided we no longer wanted to follow Him and that our way was better.

In our minds, our order of importance flipped upside down. Originally, everything was God first, man second. With the Fall, we decided to start acting like the order was: man first, God second. Even though God still belonged in first place, we started acting like we belonged in first place.

Truthfully, we still act like this all the time. Every time we know what God wants us to do and then do what we want instead, we effectively put our needs, wants, and desires above God's. We make our way higher than His. Now, some of us might *think* we don't do this, but take a look at your actions and think about it again. Do you always do what God would want you to do? Do you always even *try* to do what God would want you to do? The answer for anyone who is honest with themselves is "No."

At this point, we might protest for a minute and say, "Hold on. Why should I have to place God's desires above mine?" If you think about it, we actually spent the last two chapters answering that exact question. Very simply, we should put God first because of who He is and what He has done for us through Christ. He created us and made us beautiful. We rebelled against Him and lost much of that beauty. We became (at least partially) broken. Then, God came as a man and sacrificed Himself for us to fix the parts of us that are broken and to make the beautiful parts even more beautiful. And the whole time He is doing that, we're asking questions like, "Why should I have to follow Him?" Even when He's helping us, we're still not that interested in following. So, who really belongs in first place? God or us? When you think about it this way, the question "Why should I have to place God's desires above mine?" doesn't make much sense. We're the ones who are broken and in need of help.

And yet, we do place ourselves and our desires above God and His desires. The problem is, that is literally idolatry. *Idolatry* is putting anyone or anything in God's place. If we treat what we want as more important than what God wants, we are putting ourselves above God. We are making ourselves into our own idols.

Let me go over this again and be very specific. You want to know something that's idolatry that most of us don't think is a big deal? Selfishness. *Selfishness* is just putting ourselves first, right? Right. However, as we just discussed, we don't belong in first place, do we? No. God belongs there. So, when we act selfishly, we are committing a specific form of idolatry. We are putting ourselves in God's place and making ourselves our own gods.

Selfishness is not simply some childish attitude we have not fully outgrown. Selfishness is THE problem we all have. It is the central thing wrong with all humans. We are all selfish creatures. And we are not just selfish towards God. We regularly demonstrate that we put ourselves above other humans, too.

Of course, while every one of us is selfish, the *way* that self-ishness shows up in our lives varies from person to person. The lists of sins you see here and there in the New Testament are ways of showing how this applies to different people's situations. For example, greed is selfishness, because we are trying to get more at the expense of others. However, it's not the earning of money that is the problem. People who earn a lot of money and then give it away are not called greedy. They're called *philanthro-pists*—which literally means "lovers of mankind." Greedy people don't love mankind; they love themselves. Greed is getting more at the expense of others, and that's selfish.

You can actually look at the whole spectrum of sexual sins in the New Testament as selfish, because they are centered around putting one's own desires first. I say that for two reasons. First, if God placed limits on our sexual activity (which the New Testa-ment assumes), then any time we step past those limits, we are acting directly against God. We are putting what we want above what He wants. Second, healthy sexual activity occurs inside a relationship that seeks the good of the other person. Any time we have sex outside of a relationship that seeks the good of the other person, we are putting ourselves first. We are seeking to fulfill our own desires—possibly at the other's expense.

Now, it makes no difference if two people agree to have sex outside of a relationship that seeks the good of the other person. Consent is critical to a healthy sexual relationship, but it is not the only factor. Even if two people consent to doing something that could potentially harm the other person because it's some-thing they both want, they are still acting selfishly—even if they agree to do it together. Agreeing to act selfishly together doesn't make it any less selfish. If you're not in a relationship that seeks the good of the other person, then you're not seeking the good of the other person. That's selfish.

Moving on to another category of things, we can look at all the different forms of anger, wrath, speaking falsely about others, and gossiping as selfish. Maybe someone else has something we want, so we get mad if they have it. Or we try to set the story straight about someone else by "letting some things be known"—which may not be quite the whole truth. Sometimes, we might make fun of other people, because it makes us feel better about ourselves. Or, perhaps we hold grudges, because we think we deserve better treatment—all the while forgetting that we have been forgiven by God when we certainly didn't deserve to be.

In all of these things, we think we deserve better than we're getting, so we get mad, or bend the truth, or gossip, or put people down, or hold grudges. We are like little tyrant kings who think everyone and everything in our kingdom exists purely for ourselves. If we want something, we must have it—or off with their heads. It does not matter how much it costs others. It only matters that we get what we want. And even if we don't go as far as taking someone's head off, we still think we deserve better, and we're going to do what it takes to have just a little bit more of what we think we should have. The only difference between us and the tyrant king is one of degree.

Through our selfishness we demonstrate that we think we belong in first place, and that is the one place we do not belong. That place belongs to God. So, if we truly want to live the Christian life, we need to stop acting selfishly.

3. Start Acting Selflessly

The next thing we can do is to start acting selflessly. This sounds like a repeat of the last section, but it really isn't. If all we did was focus on not acting selfishly, we would all become hermits living in some remote place with little to no interaction with the outside world. After all, if we didn't interact with anyone, then we couldn't act selfishly towards them, right?

While that sounds technically correct, something sounds a little off, too. We're not supposed to just *not* cause problems. We're supposed to actually make the world a better place. Remember that whole "image of God" thing? We're supposed to represent God to others, and we can't do that very well by living as hermits. We have to actually be around people to represent God to people.

Simply put, the Christian life is not just about avoiding bad things; it's also about doing good things. And that's why we are talking about acting selflessly. We need to not just remove the negative; we need to add the positive. But why exactly are we supposed to act selflessly? Why is that the thing we have to do?

Think back to what we talked about in the last section—about idolatry and how God is supposed to be first and man is supposed to be second. Well, I want to break apart that second category, man, into two parts: ourselves and others. After all, it's not just God and me in this world. There are other people, too. So, where do they fit in? Well, we're supposed to reflect and represent God like Jesus did, right? That probably means it would be a good idea to start with his actions and see what he did. So, what did he do?

Think back to the cross. Christ died for us while we were working against him. We were playing for the other team, the domain of darkness. We were literally his enemies, and yet he sacrificed himself to help us. Jesus showed us what loving your enemies really means.

What happened in all of this is that Jesus placed others in a higher position than himself.[16] He acted selflessly on others' (our) behalf. So, if we are going to be the images of God, then we must live like Jesus did. That means the proper order of importance is not simply: 1) God and 2) Man. It is: 1) God, 2) Others, and 3) Self.

Now, it might be possible to explain what this means in more simple terms. I could just say, "Love God and love others." And that sounds pretty good. The only problem with breaking it down to "love God and love others," though, is that there's more to the word *"love"* than most of us realize. You see, "love" is actually a

---

16. Higher in how he treated them—not actual value

poor translation of what the New Testament is talking about. Let me explain.

Think of the way Jesus treated the poor, the lame, the blind, the sinners, the tax collectors, and the prostitutes. He acted towards them in a way no one else would. Jesus treated them with compassion, he treated them like real people and not outcasts, and he helped them. When Christianity began, there really wasn't a word that described those sorts of actions. What early Christians basically did was to take over a word that was not used much at the time and give it their own meaning. They took over the Greek word *agape* (uh-GAW-pay)—the word we translate as love.

Now, on the one hand, *love* really is the single best word to translate *agape* into English. The problem is that we English-speakers use the word *love* in a very different way than the New Testament writers did. So, when we talk about "loving others," we're often communicating something very different than the New Testament is communicating when various authors tell you to love others.

You see, in the modern West, love is directly tied to emotions. We primarily think about love as a romantic or emotional feeling. However, agape is not tied to emotions. Think about Jesus telling you to agape/love your enemies. Is his command really that you're just supposed to flip a switch in your brain and start having warm, fuzzy feelings about people who hate you? Possibly, but probably not. I think Jesus meant something else.

When Jesus was telling people to agape/love their enemies, what he meant was that we should treat them with kindness, humility, and patience. We are to treat them as we would want to be treated. Even though we have many negative emotional feelings towards them (they are our enemies, after all), we are to do the right thing for them. We shouldn't focus on changing our emotions towards our enemies. We should focus on acting selflessly towards them. Our emotions may change with time, but they are not the focus.

Our focus should be on following Jesus' example. He loved his enemies (us) when we were fighting against him. And still, he sacrificed himself to help us. Jesus is essentially saying, "I have shown you what it means to love your enemies. Now, go and do likewise."

For us to go and do likewise, we need to act selflessly toward others. I could simply say that we are supposed to love others. But if I do that, it's going to sound like we're supposed to have positive emotional feelings towards them and just try to be nice to everyone. Now, that plan probably isn't a bad one. If we truly start to care about our enemies the way Christ cared about us when we were his enemies, we might start to develop positive emotional feelings towards them. We might even start feeling compassion.

However, that's not a leap many people can make. And furthermore, the end goal isn't to simply have positive emotional feelings towards everyone around you. It's to treat them as Christ treated us. Agape/love is not about emotion; it's about action.

The real force of the word *agape/love* is that we are supposed to *do* something. We are supposed to act. And the actions we are to perform are selfless actions. We are not supposed to just sit around, not bother anyone, and try to be nice when we do happen to run into someone. We are to actively do good for those around us. Those are two very different paths, and they look very different in practice.

4. Live for Where You're Headed

In previous chapters, we talked about Christian *hope* and saw that it meant the future is different because of what Christ has done. We also saw that the afterlife is really about a relationship with God rather than simply getting into heaven. Additionally, we saw that God is in the process of renewing us into His image, and whatever path we start down in this life will be completed in the next life. If all of these things are true, there is only one rational way we can respond. We should completely refocus our lives and live for what is to come. We should aim at a *heavenly goal* (God) rather than *earthly goals* (our satisfaction or short-term happiness).

So, here's a question: "What do you live for?" Now, I don't mean, what do you *say* you live for? A lot of people will say they live for God, for their family, for being kind to others, etc. But here's the question: "Do they *really* live for those things?" Do we? At its essence, the issue is about focus. "What is our focus?"

You see, one person could be on their way to church but is really focused on talking with their friend about last night's game, the party they're both going to, or some other event. On the other hand, another person could be going to a party or a game and be more concerned with connecting with that person they know who's going through a really hard time than they are about the event itself. Which person has a more heavenly focus?

When I'm talking about your focus, I want to know: What things drive you? What things get you up in the morning or keep you up at night? What things are you looking forward to? What things do you plan for or move other things around for? These questions are meant to help you think through what the most important things in your life are.

What we really need to ask is: "Are we focused on heavenly things or earthly things? Are we more interested in knowing God and living as Christ's representatives, or are we more interested in living our lives and maybe doing a few good things along the way?" One of those is a heavenly focus, and one of those is an earthly focus.

If you try to start living a more heavenly focused life, you'll find out very quickly that not many people do. Conversations about heavenly things are not easy to get going, because most people are focused on what they call "their daily lives"—you know, work stuff, kid stuff, house stuff, social stuff . . . Basically, their *"daily lives* are all the things that they have to deal with to make it from one day to the next combined with their social activities. And anything you try to talk about that doesn't directly relate to their day-to-day lives is considered "not relevant."

But, here's the thing. Aren't our "daily lives" just the "cares of the world" that choked out the seed that fell among thorns (Matthew 13:1–23)? Aren't these just the things that steal our attention away from what truly matters And thereby, cause us to be unfruitful?

If everything we have seen up to this point is true, we probably shouldn't focus so much on our daily lives. All of the things that seem so important now will one day pass away. Yes, we have to take care of day-to-day things to get through life. But these are just that—things we have to take care of to get through life. But they are not life itself, nor are they eternal life. They are not the things that lead to renewal. We should take care of the things we have so that we can survive, but our focus should be living as the hands and feet of Christ in this world. We should be living for a purpose. Everything else is just the cares of the world.

Approximately one-sixth of the Sermon on the Mount is about *not* focusing on what we call "our daily lives." Read Matthew 6:19–34. Jesus said: "Don't store up treasures on earth, but store up treasures in heaven," "No one can serve two masters; you cannot serve both God and money," and "Don't worry about what you will eat, drink, or wear; God will take care of all of these things. Instead, pursue God and His righteousness, and all of these things will be taken care of for you."

When Jesus said no one can serve two masters, he basically meant you can only aim at one thing at a time. If you aim well and pursue your goal, you will probably hit your target. But the question is: "What are you aiming at?" Are you aiming at having a "better life?" If you are, and you hit your target, your daily life will be good, and you will earn plenty of treasures in this life. Of course, this life will end. And if Christianity is true and there is something beyond this life, then you will have wasted your life. You will have thrown away your only chance at something eternal in exchange for things that will pass away.

If, however, you aim at a heavenly target and hit your target, you will end up with something much better. You will be renewed into someone who is truly human and who knows God Himself. You will almost certainly not have the best life you could have had in this world (because you haven't been aiming at it or working towards it). But you will have gained something far better, a treasure that does not rust and cannot be stolen.

Jesus said those who wish to save their life will lose it, and those who lose their life will find it (Matthew 16:25). This is exactly what he was talking about. If you focus on having a nice life during your time on Earth, you will lose out on what you could have had: renewal into God's image and a good relationship with Him.

There is a cost to this though. You have to lose your life. You must give up this life and everything this world has to offer. But if what God has to offer is better, then you have made a wise trade.

The thing is, you cannot choose both. You cannot focus on both the heavenly life and the earthly life. You cannot focus on renewal AND on your daily life. You can only focus on one or the other. You can only have one or the other. So, which do you choose? Do you choose to focus on the earthly life or the heavenly life? Do you choose to save your life or lose it?

Like the spiral, there is no middle ground. You cannot sometimes obey God and sometimes disobey Him and think you'll make progress. Progress up or down the spiral only happens when you consistently choose one direction—whether up or down. Half-hearted attempts will get you nowhere. You're either in or you're out. But if Christianity is actually true, and everything we have talked about is true, the only option that makes sense is to live for where you're headed. Live the heavenly life.

5. Live in the World, but Live Differently

OK, so here's our situation. We are supposed to live for where we're headed; we're supposed to live in a heavenly manner. The problem is, most of the people around us are living in an earthly manner. We're not going to make sense to them. We're going to look pretty weird. People won't understand us; they'll think we're crazy. They will probably look at us and wonder, "What's up with them?" The good news is, that is precisely the question we want people to ask.

Our goal is to reflect and represent God. That is what it means for us to be His images. But what we need to do is be a reflection of something that is beyond this world, rather than simply being strange or odd. The only question is: "How do we do that?"

The most important thing we can do is to live better than we have to. If most of the people you know are unkind to someone who doesn't fit in well, be kind to that person. If it is common for everyone to fudge a little on the numbers they report at work, don't you do it, too. Be honest. When people pick sides on a religious or political issue and get super-upset at the people on the other side, try to think about things from both perspectives and be the voice of reason. You can have an opinion on controversial topics, but don't shut your eyes and ears to everyone who disagrees with you.

You might be surprised to hear this, but Jesus didn't go around preaching as much as people tend to think he did. Instead, Jesus went around *doing* things and living out his message. Then, people would ask: "What's up, Jesus? Why are you doing that?" Then, he would explain it to them.

Luke 15 is a great example of this. The whole chapter is Jesus' explanation of what he was doing in the first two verses. Tax collectors and sinners were coming to him and listening to him. And Jesus welcomed them and ate with them. But the religious leaders got upset—because these were bad people. So, Jesus told three parables to explain what he was doing: the lost sheep, the lost coin, and the lost son (the prodigal son). Jesus did things, but because those things were so different from what everyone else was doing, he had to explain himself. Living differently has that effect.

In order to represent Christ, what we need to do is live in and among everyone else. But we need to be different. We need to live better. Stop acting selfishly and start acting selflessly. If you manage to accomplish those two things, you won't need miracles or big, showy things to get people's attention. That's going to make you so different from everyone else that people will sit up and take notice. Just stop being so focused on yourself and instead, focus on others.

To accomplish this, we need to live in the world's systems rather than become separate and make our own system. To be the salt of the earth, we have to actually share life with other people. Salt can only flavor food if it's in the food. To be a light in the darkness, we have to actually be in dark places. Warning: this will not be easy, and it will be messy.

6. Focus on a Heavenly Measure of Success

Now, if you live differently than other people and show them there is a better way, what's going to happen is that it will put a light on their actions. Remember Jesus saying we are to be a light in the darkness? Well, the problem is that not everyone is going to like that. If people wanted a light on their actions, they would be seeking the light already. If they're not already doing that, then chances are they won't be thrilled about you shining a light into their dark places.

Remember, your purpose in life is to reflect and represent God. You're supposed to live like Christ. And he lived in a way that put a light on other people's actions. How did that work out for him again? Don't forget the person you're following told you to take up your cross daily. And he also said that a servant is not greater than his master; if they persecuted me, they will persecute you.

So, at best, you probably won't have success in the normal sense of the word. At worst, you'll have persecution and death. And that brings us to an important question: "How do you know if you are succeeding?" How do you know if you really are on the right path and not just crazy?

In order to have an idea of how you are doing, you need a heavenly standard of success. Your end goal as a Christian is to become renewed in God's image. When people look at you, they should think, "So that's what God is like." That means that instead of asking questions like "How much money am I making?" or "Do other people think of me as successful?", you should ask different questions.

In Colossians 3:17, Paul said, "Whatever you do, in word or deed, do everything in the name of the Lord Jesus." So, how about this: "Are you doing *everything* for the Lord Jesus?" Are you following him to the true limit of your abilities, or are you only going halfway? Are you doing everything for *Jesus*, or are you really doing it for yourself?

If you are doing everything for Jesus then you're walking in the right direction. And if you are doing everything you can and holding nothing back, then there is literally nothing more you can do. You are giving your all, and that's all you can do.

Paul said: one sows, another waters, but God makes things grow (1 Corinthians 3:7). Your job is to give everything you have to the task God has put in front of you. God's job is to make things produce fruit. Leave that up to Him. Don't get frustrated if things don't work out the way you want them to, and don't congratulate yourself if things work out really well. The question for you is: "Did you do the best you could with what God put in front of you?"

If we truly live like this, we are going to look very strange. We will pass up on many things people on the outside would grab with both hands. This will make them look at us and say, "What are you doing? Are you crazy?" It will make no sense to them why we don't live like them—why we would throw things away that others would pursue and pursue things others would throw away. But this is also what points them in a heavenly direction. The reason we live the way we do is because as Christians our goals are different.

In order to make sense of this in our own minds though, we must have a new measure of success. We should ask questions like: "Do I know God better this year than I did last year?", "Am I acting more selflessly towards others than I used to?", and "Am I doing everything for God rather than for myself?" But again, this is going to make us look strange to people who don't live this way, and we are going to miss out on a lot of the things.

This is why the question "Is Christianity true?" is so important. This is why we spent so much time talking about arguments for the existence of God and the truth of Christianity. If Christianity is true, then it makes sense to follow Christ and ignore what this world considers success. If Christianity is not true, then following Christ is foolish.

You have a choice in front of you—the same choice that Jesus put in front of people who listened to him. Are you going to pick up your cross and follow him? Are you going to lose your life for his sake? You cannot pursue heavenly things and earthly things. You can only have one goal. You have to choose. Just know that if you choose to follow Christ and to live for heavenly goals, success is going to look very different. You will likely fail by earthly standards if you choose to ignore them and focus on heavenly standards.

7. Share Revelation and Renewal

What does it mean to *share revelation*? In the first section of this chapter, we talked about several sources of revelation. What is really interesting is that as we reflect God more, we actually start to become one of those sources of revelation. If we're doing what we should be doing, people will be able to look at us and see God (assuming we've been following God and spiraling up rather than ignoring or rejecting Him). By reflecting God, we become a source of revelation to others.

Revelation is what begins our spiral. Just like revelation begins our spirals, revelation begins others' spirals, too. That means that by revealing God, we get other people's spirals going. So, to the extent that we reflect God, we increase the amount of revelation of God in this world and get those around us moving. We are sharing in the work God is doing in this world.

So, what does it mean to *share renewal*? One part of sharing renewal is helping others on the path to renewal. We do this by walking a right path ourselves and showing them what the process of renewal looks like in us. It's not about being perfect; it's about moving in the right direction. We need to acknowledge our faults, deal with them, and move forward and upward. We shouldn't try to push the people around us in the right direction. We should try to inspire them. We shouldn't leave them to walk the path alone. We should get down in the mess and help them where they are. Instead of saying, "Go that way," say, "Come with me."

Another part of sharing renewal is making the world around us a better place. But before we can even attempt to make the world a better place, we have to become people who are capable of bringing about a change that is actually positive. It does no good to change the world if we change it for the worse. We need to change it for the better. But what is better? What does that look like?

The only way to answer that question is by becoming people who know God and reflect Him. Otherwise, we'll be remaking the world in our own image. We'll be remaking it the way *we* think it should look rather than the way *God* thinks it should look. And if we're still broken people, that's not going to go very well. We need to remove the log from our own eye so that we can see clearly to remove the speck from our neighbor's eye. If we want to make the world better, we have to start by becoming people who are capable of doing that work.

This means we need to respond correctly to revelation and begin the renewal process. If we did nothing for the next ten years but learn as much as we could about God and fix as much as we could in our own lives that is broken, we would not be wasting our time. Honestly, there is no better place to start. After all, we cannot share what we do not have. If we aren't people who know God Himself and actually look like Him, how could we possibly represent Him to others? How can we fix the world if we're not fixed ourselves?

It is a massive task for us to get our own lives together and live in a world that operates very differently. That's why I said that we would not be wasting our time if we focused on nothing else for the next ten years. This is not a one-month or even a one-year thing. Becoming someone who actually reflects God will take everything we have. Why do you think Jesus told people they had to lose their lives if they wanted to follow him? That may mean you die in the process of following him. But far more often it means that you die to your current life and begin a new life. You can begin that journey on a single day, but it takes time to make progress down the path. And until you have made some progress down the path, how can you tell someone else, "This is the way to go. Follow me."

Revealing and representing God is our vocation as Christians. It is our job. And it is the only job we have that really matters, because it is the only one that has a product that lasts eternally.

The way we begin to do our job is by receiving revelation and renewal. We need to get ourselves together first before we will be in a position to help others. But the stronger we become, the better we will be able to help others. As we become more and more renewed in the image of God, we will become more are more capable of helping in God's work. And helping in God's work is what the Christian life is all about.

Conclusion

Let's review the points we discussed in this chapter. They are:

1. <u>Receive Revelation and Renewal</u>

   Creation, our gut feeling about right and wrong, and the Bible are all sources of God's revelation. *Receiving revelation* is about paying attention when God is talking. *Receiving renewal* is about acting on what God has said.

2. <u>Stop Acting Selfishly</u>

   We place ourselves above God and others. We think we're the most important thing in the world. We need to stop acting like we belong in first place, because we don't belong there. God does.

3. <u>Start Acting Selflessly</u>

   The order of importance we should have is: God first, others second, and self, third. To *love* someone is to act selflessly on their behalf. That means we need to treat others how we would want to be treated and act selflessly on their behalf.

4. <u>Live for Where You're Headed</u>

   What do you live for, really? What is your focus? Are you focused on your daily life, or are you focused on representing Christ? Do you want the things that give you a nice life or the things that lead to renewal for yourself and others? We should aim at a heavenly goal rather than an earthly goal.

5. Live in the World, but Live Differently

If we live for where we're headed, we are going to look different. But that's what we want. We want to live in a manner that points people upward. We do this by living in the world's systems but living better than we have to.

6. Focus on a Heavenly Measure of Success

We probably won't have success by earthly standards, because we're not even working toward the same goals. Since we have different goals, we need to ask different questions. We should ask: "Do I know God better this year than I did last year?", "Am I acting more selflessly towards others than I used to?", and "Am I doing everything for Christ rather than for myself?" If we can answer yes to questions like these, then we're on the right path.

7. Share Revelation and Renewal

The more we receive revelation and renewal, the more we reflect and represent God. As a result, we start to become a source of revelation to others. People will be able to look at us and see God. And then, we can truly share renewal with others and make the world around us a better place.

In this chapter, we have looked at the last link in the chain that is the Christian worldview. To review, these four links are: 1) The Truth of Christianity, 2) The Person and Work of Christ, 3) Beliefs and Actions, and 4) The Christian Life.

Everything in these last four chapters is connected. According to Christianity, the way we should live on a day-to-day basis is based on true facts about the world, and the way the world actually is leads directly to our actions. Everything in Christianity is connected from top to bottom and from start to finish.

Because of this, we cannot simply make Christianity whatever we want it to be. It is what it is. Now, it could be true, or it could be false. If Christianity is true, then the world looks one way. If Christianity is false, then it looks another way. If Christianity is true, then we have the responsibility of representing God to the rest of the world. If Christianity is false, then none of this matters.

The result of this is two wildly different paths. They may seem similar if you're looking at people who call themselves Christians but don't really live for it. However, actually reordering your priorities and living for a new purpose is something completely different. If you start walking down that path, your life will change rapidly. But should you walk down that path?

Unfortunately, this is not an easy choice to make. Certainly, if Christianity is true, then the choice is easy—at least if we're considering it in a vacuum. But we're not considering it in a vacuum, are we? This isn't an academic exercise we think about in the comfort of our home and choose without consequence. There are serious consequences to which option we choose—in both directions.

Furthermore, there is no middle ground. We cannot halfway follow Christianity. That is to tell God that we only sometimes want to listen to Him—only when it suits us. God is not there for us to use when we want and cast aside when we don't. He won't put up with that. We're either going to listen to Him and follow Him or we're not.

Christianity is true . . . or not. We are going to follow God with our whole hearts . . . or not. The path of accepting Christianity and the path of rejecting it look very different and which option we choose matters. And there are consequences to both choices. How we live shows which path we choose.

CHAPTER 6

The Big Picture

Introduction

We have spent the last four chapters looking at the four links of the Christian worldview in detail. In the final chapter, we're going to pull together the threads from everything we have discussed so far and finally return to the story of Jesus and Pilate. But before we do that, we need to briefly take a look at the big picture.

Christianity is the turning point in the story of God and man. Up till now, we have been looking at each part of that turning point in detail. But we haven't spent much time on the story itself. So, let's look at the story of God and man and see how Christianity fits in.

There are four main elements in the story of God and man: 1) God, 2) Christ, 3) Creation, and 4) Man. Now, this is not everything in the story or everything in existence. But these are the leading actors (God, Christ, and man) as well as the stage on which everything takes place (creation). In this chapter, we will look at each one of these parts separately and then see how they fit together. Some of this will be review; some of this will be new; But the way we are going to cover it will help you take a fresh look at it.

1. God

There Is a God

There is no more foundational statement when we are describing Christianity than saying, "There is a god." That single statement has an enormous impact on the way we view and describe the world around us. If there is a god, then we will describe the world as created rather than existing by chance. Miracles, answers to prayer, an afterlife, and real purpose (rather than purpose we create for ourselves) are all now possible. Precisely, what the world looks like depends on which god we're talking about. But we can only talk about things like creation, miracles, and answered prayers if there actually is a god. They make no sense on atheism.

However, we should not believe in a god simply because we want these things. If atheism is true and there is no god, then that is simply the way things are. So be it. I, for one, want to believe what is actually true. I do not want to trick myself into believing something just because it makes me feel good. Besides, that wouldn't work for very long anyway. The truth will eventually make itself known. And if I have been living in a way that doesn't line up with how things actually are, there will be consequences. Tricking ourselves into believing something that makes us feel good is basically sacrificing our future for our present. That never ends well.

Another reason why God existing is so important to Christianity is because it shapes what we do. If there is a god, then we can speak of moral values as real things rather than things that merely come out of our culture or things that we create for ourselves. If there is a god, then it is possible that everything is not relative. Some things, at least, really are right and wrong. It is right to love your neighbor as yourself. It is wrong to treat other people like tools or objects. If there is no god, then we can only speak of actions as pleasant (or not) or useful (or not). But there is no real right and wrong. It is: "To each his own"—whatever that may be.

It would be worth our time to look into the question, "Is there a god?" After all, the truth of Christianity is the first link in the chain of the Christian worldview. So, the existence of a god is critical. If there is no god, there is no Christianity. If there is a god, then Christianity *might* be true (depending on which god we're talking about). Finding out whether there are any good reasons to think that a god actually exists can help us figure out whether we have the right view of the world or not.

There Is One God—the God of Abraham, Isaac, and Jacob
It is important to understand that when we talk about Christianity, we are not talking about some generic, prepackaged god that could fit into any sort of mold we might like. No. The God of Christianity is the same God Genesis speaks of when it says, "In the beginning, God created the heavens and the earth." The God of Christianity is the same God who made a covenant with Abraham and confirmed it with his son Isaac and his son Jacob. The God of Christianity is the same God we see interacting with the people of Israel in the Old Testament and who refers to Himself as "I am."

Certainly, Jews and Christians have some different ideas about the nature of God. However, what I want to make clear is that when Christians refer to *God*, we are talking about the Jewish God. There is no different God of the New Testament. Christians believe that God has given further revelation about Himself through Christ, but we still mean to refer to the same God. Christianity cannot be separated from Judaism. Christianity is the climax of the Jewish story of God and man.

God Is Ultimately Responsible for Everything
If we had to pick a place and say, "The buck stops here," we would point to God and say the buck stops with God. God is ultimately

responsible for everything, even though He does delegate responsibility to humans. The responsibility we have for our own lives, for how we treat others, and for how we take care of the world around us is something we have because God has given it to us.

Humanity's proper focus in life is on God. We are to know His will and follow the path He puts in front of us. It is God who rescues us from the domain of darkness and transfers us to the kingdom of Christ. God builds the believer up, judges humanity, and is the one we should thank for everything good we have received. God began all things and will see them to their conclusion. He is ultimately responsible for everything.

2. Christ

Christ Is How We Meet God

Christ is how we know what God is like. He is the full revelation of God. That means that while we may get glimpses or ideas of God from other sources, Christ is the full picture. There is no clearer picture of God than the person and work of Christ.

Beyond how we know God, Christ is how we can approach God and interact with Him. We humans live in hostility to God and want to do things our own way rather than God's way. In order to make the relationship with God right, humanity needs help. Christ is the one who puts humans back in good standing with God and on the path to renewal.

Humans have always been curious about God. We have imagined what God or the gods might be like and what he, she, it, or they might want us to do. However, Christianity claims that it is not a man-made attempt to reach up to God. Christianity claims that as Christ, God has reached down to man. If this claim is true, then it means man cannot possibly know God better or meet Him more effectively than by the God-given way of bridging the gap between the two parties.

Christ Is Responsible for Creation

Christ is the one who created all things originally. All things in heaven and on earth, all things visible and invisible, and even all the powers that be (whether earthly or heavenly) that choose to fight against God were created by Christ. He is the beginning of creation, and he is its author. He is the uncreated creator.

However, Christianity also teaches that Christ was born as a human, Jesus of Nazareth. He lived a human life and even died as a human. In Jesus, the divine and the human came together in a single person. *How* exactly that works is a much larger question (which goes beyond what we are covering in this book). But *that* it happened is an essential part of Christianity. Christ existed without creation, created all things, and then stepped into creation as a human.

At present, Christ is in the process of renewing creation. At some point, after Christ originally created everything, things went wrong. The reason Christ came as a man, died, and rose from the dead was to put those things back on the right path. Currently, Christ is actively working through those humans who follow him to fix what is wrong with creation. He will finally complete the renewal of creation at a point in the future in which everything will be returned to the way it should be.

Christ Died on a Cross and Rose from the Dead

Like the claim that God exists, Christianity claims that Jesus actually died on a cross and then actually rose from the dead. Paul said that if Christ is not raised then your faith is worthless and you are still in your sins (1 Corinthians 15:17). The resurrection of Jesus is so central to Christianity that Paul can say that if it did not happen, then Christianity is false.

What makes this interesting is that the statement "Jesus of Nazareth rose from the dead after dying on a cross" is a historical statement. Certainly, there are many theological implications, but first and foremost, this is a *historical statement*. That means we can check to see if it actually happened. We can read the primary sources, look for facts, and try to figure out how best to explain those facts. If we really want to know whether Christianity is true or not, it is worth our time to look into the question, "Did Jesus *really* rise from the dead?"

The reason the resurrection of Jesus is so important is because it makes the reconciliation and renewal of humanity possible. Christ created everything perfectly, but we fell from our original perfection and harmony with God. We became flawed and hostile toward God. Because of Christ's resurrection, he can repair the separation that exists between God and man and fix what is wrong with us. All of creation will be reconciled to God—the battle between the creator and all those who work against him will end. However, those who follow Christ will experience renewal in addition to reconciliation. We will one day fully reflect our creator and be remade into true humans.

3. Creation

Original Creation

In the beginning, when God created the heavens and the earth, everything was good and all things were in harmony with their creator. Think about all the problems in the world today and everything that is wrong with it. Now, imagine that none of those problems ever existed. Imagine there was no evil, pain, suffering, anger, greed, or any of the other things we wish were not a part of this world. Everything and everyone was good.

Part of what this harmony meant is that all humans had the proper orientation toward their creator. Humans recognized who their creator was and followed His commands. This is how we were meant to operate. Just as a machine that is operating outside the way in which it was designed can be said to be dysfunctional and possibly broken, a human operating outside the way in which he or she was designed can be said to be dysfunctional and possibly broken. We were designed to operate in harmony with our creator and according to his specifications.

Fall of Creation

With the Fall, everything changed. Everything that was good became tainted, and humanity became a shadow of what it once was. At this point, all of the things that are wrong with this world today became a regular part of it. Life became hard, work became toil, and death became a reality.

Additionally, the harmony that existed between creator and creation was lost. Humanity became hostile toward its creator—whether by actively working against Him or by simply refusing to obey His commands. Whereas humanity once operated according to its original specifications, it now began to operate in a dysfunctional way. We stopped operating the way we were meant to.

Something else happened though that set humanity on a different path. Previously, we could have described all humans as having been a part of the kingdom of Christ. With the Fall, a second kingdom began to exist: the domain of darkness. This is basically the exact opposite of the kingdom of Christ. Instead of living in harmony with their creator, someone who is part of the domain of darkness is hostile toward Him. Instead of functioning well, that person is dysfunctional. And what makes things worse is that with the Fall, this became humanity's default position. Humans do not have to choose to be a part of the domain of darkness. We are born into it.

Renewal of Creation

Fortunately, the story does not end with the Fall. Christ has been working to fix what went wrong with creation. Through his death and resurrection, Christ made a way for humans to step out of the domain of darkness and back into his kingdom. Those who take this option will no longer live in hostility toward their creator, nor will they function poorly. They will begin to be renewed during this life And when they cross into the next life, they will become perfect and complete, lacking nothing. The only thing required to make this happen is for humans to respond to the same call Jesus made in the Gospels: "Follow me."

Obviously, not everyone chooses to follow Christ. That does not mean, however, that the domain of darkness will continue to exist forever and God will tolerate His creation to exist in hostility toward Him. The domain of darkness will be destroyed and its members will be returned to their proper creational order. That means they will be removed from the position they have given themselves (first place) and be placed where they belong (after their creator). God first, man second.

However, while everyone will one day be returned to their proper creational order (God first, man second), some return willingly and some don't. All humanity is born into the domain of darkness, and all humanity will one day be in line with their creator. Those who follow Christ willingly will be renewed into the perfect and complete creations they were meant to be. Those who don't, won't.

4. Man

Everyone Is Beautiful and Everyone Is Broken
Each of us begins our life as a mixed bag. Some parts of us are beautiful. Some parts of us are broken. Some people don't like to think about the fact that we are all beautiful, and some people don't like to think about the fact that we are all broken. But the truth is, we are all both of those things.

The problem is that we were all created to be perfect beings. We are all a few steps down from where we should be. We are not perfect. We are imperfect. And that is the problem Christ is solving. Christ is fixing the imperfection in humanity and renewing us into perfect beings—true humans. Christ is working to fix our broken parts and make our beautiful parts even more beautiful.

Christ Renews Man

Christ working to renew humanity means that he is remaking those of us who follow him into the image of God. He is remaking us into good representatives of God. If God is loving, then we must be loving in order to represent God well. If God is fair, just, and selfless, then we must also be fair, just, and selfless if we are going to represent God well.

Renewal is a process that begins in this life and will be completed in the next life. No one is going to look perfect now. That will not happen in this life. Someone who follows Christ should, however, become more and more perfected with time. This may not happen on a daily basis, but as you look at a person's life over the course of months and years, you should see an upward trend.

This process will finally be completed at the end of this life. When the believer dies and goes to be with Christ, Christ will finish his work of renewal and the believer will become fully renewed and truly human. That does not imply that everyone will be the same. It only means that each one of us will be without fault as the unique and beautiful individuals we were meant to be.

Renewal Happens in the Church

Some portion of humanity is being renewed, and this group is called the *Church* (big-C Church, not little-c church). The Church is the group of those people who are part of Christ's team. They are those who have answered his call to "follow me," and they are the ones who are being renewed.

In talking about the Church, it is important to understand that this is a relational, spiritual, and moral category all rolled into one. The repair of our relationship with God through Christ happens in the Church. Our renewal into the image of God happens in the Church. Forgiveness for all the wrong that we have done happens in the Church. The reason for this is that *Church* is the word for those who are connected to Christ and are on his team. And because Christ is the only place where these things can be found, the only place where we can expect to find them is in the Church.

Christianity and the Story of God and Man

In the beginning, God created the heavens and the earth. Everything was good and existed in harmony with its creator. At some point, humanity fell and lost the goodness it once had and the harmony it once enjoyed with its creator. Christianity is what God has done through Christ to fix what went wrong with humanity. Christianity is the turning point in the story of God and man. It is how God has acted decisively to bring His once good and now broken creation to a good and unbroken conclusion.

In this story, humanity was created in the image of God. Since original creation, we have fallen from that image and no longer accurately represent God or look like the perfect and complete creations we originally were. Through Christ, we can become renewed into people who are truly human. Alternatively, we could continue down our current path and lose what humanity we have left.

Humans, therefore, find themselves at a fork in the road. The main story has already been written, the paths are laid out before us, and the end of both is certain. Yet, each of us has two paths in front of us. The only question that remains is, "Which one will we take?" Will we go our own way and do what we think is best? Or, will we follow Christ and choose the path of revelation and renewal?"

CHAPTER 7

Revelation and Renewal

Jesus and Pilate

In the first chapter of this book, we looked at Jesus' trial before Pilate. I told you that it gave us a good picture of what the Christian life is like and that we would return to it in the last chapter of the book. Well, this is the last chapter; so, let's take a look at what happened and see what it tells us about the Christian life.

In Jesus' trial before Pilate, there are four main actors. They are: 1) Jesus, 2) Pilate, 3) the religious leaders, and 4) the crowd. These individuals and groups were real, historical people in first century Israel. However, they also represent people who are present in every day and age. We will meet these people in our journeys, and from time to time, we will be one of them. Let's take a look at them—in reverse order.

The crowd is simply the mob. They are easily influenced and their opinions change with what they've had for breakfast. Unfortunately, that does not stop them from chanting and shouting at the top of their lungs for whatever position they hold this minute. Maybe the crowd is cheering for you, and maybe it's calling for your head. But the crowd's opinions are rarely based on anything solid. Don't be the crowd, and don't pay too much attention to the crowd.

The religious leaders are the bad guys in this particular scenario. But they're not always the bad guys; the bad guy changes. Sometimes it's a religious group, sometimes it's a political party, sometimes it's a country, sometimes it's an individual, and sometimes it's a group. The bad guy changes all the time and unfortunately, many of us have played the bad guy in our own lives from time to time.

The bad guy is actively working to cause evil and chaos—even though bad guys often don't realize that's what they're doing. Bad guys should be actively opposed. You ignore the crowd; you stand against bad guys.

The first two groups, the crowd and the bad guys, are important for us to be aware of and respond to appropriately. However, they're not terribly interesting. The most interesting character in this whole scene is Pilate, because he is a mixed bag.

You see, some part of Pilate wants to do good. When we looked at Jesus' trial, we saw that he legitimately tried to get Jesus off the hook for a while. He knew Jesus was innocent, and he didn't want to condemn an innocent man to a horrible death. At this point, Pilate really was trying to do the right thing.

However, the bad guys were able to use the crowd (by stirring them up) to change the situation so Pilate could not simply say, "Is Jesus innocent or guilty? He's innocent. OK, I'm going to let him go." By exciting the crowd and twisting the situation, the bad guys put Pilate in a situation where it was either Jesus or Pilate—one of them was going to die.

When everything was nice and easy, Pilate was willing to do the right thing. But when his own neck was on the line, things changed. Would Pilate let an innocent man off the hook when it cost him nothing? Sure. Why not? Would Pilate die to save the life of an innocent man he didn't even know (and may not have liked if he had)? No. Pilate would not do that.

In this scene, Pilate is the character who is most like us. Most of us will do the right thing if it doesn't cost us anything. But what happens when our own neck is on the line? Are we willing to help someone else if it costs us personally? Are we willing to do the right thing even if it will result in our own suffering and/ or death?

Those are hard questions to answer honestly. Most of us would like to say, "Yes, I would do the right thing no matter what it costs me." But while we would like to say that, we know that the real world is harder than that. Saying you'd do the right thing no matter what is one thing. Doing it is something entirely different.

From time to time, all of us will find ourselves in Pilate's situation. We will be put between a rock and a hard place—possibly by the bad guys and possibly because that's just how things happened to work out. But we will all have to make the choice: "Will I do the right thing, even if I won't benefit from it, and even if it costs me personally?"

From a Christian perspective, Pilate made the wrong choice. The Christian life is a selfless life. Pilate put himself first. Certainly, that's what comes naturally to us, but the Christian life is about being something more. We are meant to be more than the mixed bag of good and evil that Pilate was. We are supposed to be on our way to true humanity.

By contrast, Jesus shows us how we should act in a difficult situation. He was in a similar situation to Pilate, but he made the right choice. According to Christianity, Jesus had to suffer and die in order to fix what went wrong with humanity. In his case, though, the people he was dying for weren't innocent. The people he was helping had actually done wrong things and many were actively working against him.

Jesus did the right thing—even though it cost him personally. Pilate did the wrong thing, *because* doing the right thing would cost him personally. That, right there, is the essence of the choice we each will have to make many times in our lives. Will we do the right thing, even if it costs us personally? Or will we do the wrong thing, because doing the right thing will cost us personally?

Spiritual Progress

If we are honest with ourselves, many of us probably act a little bit too much like Pilate. So, what do we do about that? How do we become better people? How do we become less like Pilate and more like Jesus? Fortunately, there are concrete steps we can take to do that. Here they are:

Let God Provide the Direction

The first thing to understand is that God provides the direction in our lives. We can make plans, but these are only useful as long as God has given us the freedom to be creative in whatever area we happen to be in. He often does this, but we need to remember that we are walking a path that we cannot see. Just because certain sections of the trail are well-lit and free from dangers doesn't mean the rest of it will be. We neither know where the trail is going; nor do we know how, when, and why we should walk the particular way He is telling us to walk. But if Christianity is true, and God really is who Christianity says He is, then we should trust that He knows what He's doing.

As part of guiding us along our path, from time to time, God will bring us somewhere that is meant to reshape us. Sometimes, God will teach us how to trust Him. He often does this by putting us in difficult situations and giving us no other good option but to trust Him. Sometimes, God will bring one of our moral shortcomings to our attention. Often this happens gently, even if it's not fun. But if we have ignored Him in the past, He might try to get our attention in a more dramatic and less pleasant way. Sometimes, God tells us to stay where we are when we'd rather go somewhere else. And sometimes, God tells us to go somewhere else when we'd rather stay where we are.

In general, it is not easy to follow God. Sometimes, the path is easy; but other times, it is exceedingly difficult. But the more closely we follow God and the better we're able to keep up with the pace He sets, the more interesting the places He can take us become. Our lives begin to have more significance, and we begin to have a greater positive impact on the world around us. And in the process, we become more human—as humans were always meant to be.

The way we do this is by learning to follow God and by doing the absolute best we can with whatever He puts in front of us. But we are still left with a big question: "How do we know when God is speaking to us?"

Learn What Scripture Says

Knowing what Scripture says is the first and most important part of knowing if God is really speaking to us. If what we think we're hearing doesn't sound like what we read in the Bible, then God probably isn't speaking to us. On the other hand, if what we're hearing does sound similar to what's in the Bible, then God might be trying to tell us something.

For example, if we think God is telling us to do the right thing in a difficult situation and to trust Him to work it out, then it's helpful to know that this is a recurring theme in Scripture. Scripture regularly emphasizes the need for faith. On the other hand, if we think God is telling us that everything is fine with our lives and we can just carry on doing whatever we're doing, then we are not hearing from God. Humans may be beautiful, but we are also broken. Scripture talks about this *a lot*.

These are really simple examples, and many of the things that we will have to deal with in our own lives will be more complicated. But we cannot handle the complicated until we have mastered the simple. Mastery of a skill requires mastery of the fundamentals.

Furthermore, the reason that the simple lessons are repeated again and again in the Bible is because they are not easy to learn.

Just because something is simple to understand does not mean it is simple to do (like doing the right thing—even if it will cost you personally). The reason the simple lessons are so often repeated is because we all have trouble with them.

Walking with God is dynamic. It is not following a set pattern of steps or clinging to a strict set of rules. However, in Scripture, we have been given the basics—the things we all need to know to get going. And we have examples of people who have walked with God in the past (as well as those who have ignored Him). We will have a lot more success if we learn from others' successes and failures and don't have to repeat all the lessons they had to learn.

Be Courageous

It is not easy to follow God. Whether following God means pursuing a new direction in life, dealing with a moral shortcoming, or learning a lesson He gives us; it will take strength, effort, and courage to respond correctly. Doing the right thing when it costs nothing is easy. Pilate could walk that path. Doing the right thing no matter what it costs us is hard. That's the path Jesus walked. And that's the path he calls us to walk with him.

It is important to understand that we are not attempting to renew ourselves. Following the path God puts in front of us is what will change us. When God takes us somewhere, He is deciding what parts of us need to be worked on. By doing the best we can to learn the lessons God gives us or to go where He tells us to go, we are letting Him renew us rather than trying to renew ourselves.

However, this is not a passive process. We do not get to sit back and just let Him work without doing anything. We also don't get to take control and remake ourselves however we see fit. Neither one will work.

To let God renew us, we need to let Him decide what parts of us need to be worked on. Then, once we know what He wants us to do, our job is to do everything we can to follow the path He has put in front of us. This will often include some things we *really* don't want to do. But that's what we signed up for. Following God is simple, but it's not easy. How much God can do with us is primarily limited by how much we resist Him. If we want God to do something amazing with us and through us, it will take both strength and courage to follow Him.

People like to say God will not give you more than you can handle. That is false. God will absolutely give you more than you can handle. But He will not give you more than you can handle . . . with His help.

God intends for us to rely on Him. We are not meant to do this on our own. And so the path that God puts before us will be filled with things that are beyond our ability. Walking the Christian path requires both courage to tackle the impossible and faith that God will help us through it.

Revelation and Renewal

God's ultimate purpose for us is to renew us into His image. The clearest picture we have of God is the person of Jesus. When we look at Jesus, we are meant to say, "Oh, that's what God is like." Our job as humans is to do the same thing as Jesus (only in a smaller way). When people look at us, they should say, "Oh, that's what God is like."

Currently, we don't reflect or represent God very well. At best, people *sometimes* look at us and say, "Oh, that's what God is like." In order to be good images and representatives of God, we are going to need some work. In order to be truly human, something is going to have to change. There are four steps necessary to make that happen. They are:

1. Receive Revelation—To live as the image of God is to reflect and represent God in your daily life. To do that, you have to know what God is like—so you can represent Him

well. *Receiving revelation* means getting to know who God is.

2. <u>Receive Renewal</u>—Walk the path God has put in front of you. God knows what each of us needs to become renewed. He made humans in the first place; He ought to know how to remake us. Let God shape you by walking the path He puts in front of you. And once you know the direction He wants you to go, pursue it with your whole heart. Be courageous, and don't hold anything back.

3. <u>Share Revelation</u>—As you become a better person and more truly human, you will start to look more like Jesus. Many people never pick up a Bible, but they watch people who do. The more you look like Jesus, the more you become living revelation to those around you.

4. <u>Share Renewal</u>—Whatever God has put in front of you, do that. Wherever God has placed you, make a positive difference. Once you have experienced renewal in your own life, you know what it is like. Bring that same renewal to the world around you.

www.ingramcontent.com/pod-product-compliance
Lightning Source LLC
Chambersburg PA
CBHW071943100426

42737CB00046BA/1996